AF898107

"*The Wealth Trap* is a valuable resource for families who want to go beyond plans to protect generational wealth and raise builders who live lives of purpose and meaning by creating value for themselves and others. Connor and Taylor offer a practical playbook for helping the next generation form character, capability, and a culture of contribution that lasts."

—**Brian Hooks,** chairman and CEO of Stand Together

"Most books about family wealth focus on protecting your money. This one focuses on protecting your kids by turning them into the kind of people who don't need protecting. *The Wealth Trap* is the book I wish every successful parent would read before it's too late."

—**Garrett Gunderson,** *New York Times* bestselling author

"*The Wealth Trap* focuses on what many ultra-wealthy parents miss until they learn the hard way: that your character and values are more important to pass on than money. Without them, money will destroy a family. With them, you can build wealth and have a fulfilling life."

—**Richard Wilson,** president and founder of Family Office Club

PRAISE FOR

The Wealth Trap

"For over a decade, my wife and I wrestled with a burden heavier than building our wealth: How do we steward these resources faithfully without ruining our children and grandchildren? Giving it all away felt like abandoning God's call; hoarding it risked destroying our family. We devoured books and consulted dozens of wealthy families who'd walked this path before us. *The Wealth Trap* stood out as the clearest guide—equipping children with a meaningful mission to protect and fulfill, rather than liquid assets that erode character. It's now required reading for our trustees and beneficiaries."

—Jeffrey Harmon, serial entrepreneur and co-founder of Angel Studios

"Most books on raising kids are fluff. This one isn't. Connor and Taylor get to an uncomfortable truth: Wealth can destroy the very traits that created it. If you've made money and have kids, this is your problem. Read this book and do the work."

—Sam Parr, co-host of the *My First Million* and *Moneywise* podcasts

"Curious how to foster generational builders and leaders? This book is a must-read for any family that wants to compound their human capital."

—Jake Schutt, head of family office for Parallel Advisors

The Wealth Trap

THE BLUEPRINT TO RAISE
BUILDERS, NOT BENEFICIARIES

CONNOR BOYACK
& TAYLOR ADAMS

AN INC.
ORIGINAL

This publication is designed to provide accurate and authoritative information in regard to the subject matter covered. It is sold with the understanding that the publisher and author are not engaged in rendering legal, accounting, or other professional services. Nothing herein shall create an attorney-client relationship, and nothing herein shall constitute legal advice or a solicitation to offer legal advice. If legal advice or other expert assistance is required, the services of a competent professional should be sought.

An Inc. Original
New York, New York
www.anincoriginal.com

Copyright © 2026 Connor Boyack and Taylor Adams

All rights reserved.

Thank you for purchasing an authorized edition of this book and for complying with copyright law. No part of this book may be reproduced, stored in a retrieval system, used for training artificial intelligence technologies or systems, or transmitted by any means, electronic, mechanical, photocopying, recording, or otherwise, without written permission from the copyright holder.

This work is being published under the *An Inc. Original* imprint by an exclusive arrangement with *Inc. Magazine. Inc. Magazine* and the *Inc.* logo are registered trademarks of Mansueto Ventures, LLC. The *An Inc. Original* logo is a wholly owned trademark of Mansueto Ventures, LLC.

Distributed by Greenleaf Book Group

For ordering information or special discounts for bulk purchases, please contact Greenleaf Book Group at PO Box 91869, Austin, TX 78709, 512.891.6100.

Design and composition by Greenleaf Book Group and Jonathan Lewis
Cover design by Tiago Pereira

Publisher's Cataloging-in-Publication data is available.

Print ISBN: 978-1-63909-079-2

eBook ISBN: 978-1-63909-080-8

To offset the number of trees consumed in the printing of our books, Greenleaf donates a portion of the proceeds from each printing to the Arbor Day Foundation. Greenleaf Book Group has replaced over 50,000 trees since 2007.

Printed in the United States of America on acid-free paper

26 27 28 29 30 31 32 33 10 9 8 7 6 5 4 3 2 1

First Edition

Contents

Foreword

by Tony Robbins

There's a fear that successful people almost never talk about. It's not the fear of failure. It's not the fear of losing what they've built. It's the quiet, persistent fear that the very wealth they worked so hard to create might be the thing that destroys their children.

I've seen it thousands of times. Parents who built empires, who started with nothing and created extraordinary lives, who mastered every challenge the world threw at them—and who lie awake at night terrified that their kids will never know what it means to struggle, to earn, to build something of their own. They've given their children every advantage, and now they wonder if those advantages have become a curse.

This is deeply personal for me. I have five kids and five grandkids. Every day, when I look at my five-year-old daughter, I think about how to make sure she grows up grounded. I grew up dirt poor. She's growing up in a world I couldn't have imagined. Recently, we stayed at a friend's $175 million home in Bel Air—35,000 square feet of architectural brilliance. When we came back to our place in Palm Beach, she looked around and said, "Daddy, how come we live in such a small house?" Keep in mind, we have a 25,000-square-foot home on the ocean! And I thought: *I've really got to work to keep this kid grounded.*

That's the challenge, isn't it? How do you raise children who understand the value of creation when they've never had to create out of necessity? How do you instill hunger in a world of abundance?

Here's what I've learned over the past half a century working with families at every level: The biggest challenge in life isn't stress. It's not pressure. It's that most people are *managing* their lives instead of *creating* them. They're trying to make a living rather than design one. And when you're just managing, just maintaining, just trying to hold on to what you have—that's when the stress becomes unbearable. But when you're creating something? Creating joy, creating love, creating a business, creating a family? All that stress disappears. We're made by a Creator, and we're designed to create. When we do, we come alive.

The families I've seen thrive across generations are the ones who figured this out. They raised creators. Builders. People who understand that wealth isn't something you protect—it's a resource you deploy in service of something bigger than yourself.

Figuring out how to do that—how to grow our human capital alongside our financial capital—is easier said than done. That's what makes this book so valuable. Connor Boyack and Taylor Adams are among the most important thinkers working on the problems that will define the next century, and in *The Wealth Trap*, they've delivered something extraordinary: a real answer to how human beings flourish when abundance removes the need to struggle.

What you're about to read isn't a parenting book or wealth planning guide. It's a complete reorientation of what we're actually passing on to our children. Not money. Not opportunity. Not comfort. But the capacity to create value for others, which is the only wealth that truly compounds across generations.

I'll be honest: When I read this, I found myself thinking, *This is exactly what families need. This is what* I *need*. The clarity. The practicality. The unflinching honesty about what's really at stake. Connor and Taylor understand that you can't lecture your children into becoming builders. You can't design a trust document that produces character. You have to create the conditions—the experiences, the struggles, the opportunities—that forge it. And this book shows you how.

So if you're a parent who's achieved success but fears what that success might do to your children, if you're a grandparent who wants to leave behind more than money, if you're someone who understands that the real inheritance isn't wealth but the capacity to create it—then don't just read this book. Study it. Apply it. Let it change not just how you raise your children, but how you live your own life.

Because this isn't a book about protecting your family's wealth. It's a book about redeeming it—transforming abundance from a threat into fuel for lives of creation and contribution.

Your children are watching. The future is waiting.

Step in. Step up. The journey starts here.

Tony Robbins
America's #1 Life and Business Strategist
#1 *New York Times* Best-selling Author
February 2026

Preface

This book's thesis is simple but provocative: Affluent families struggle immensely to raise their children in abundance, and most of the advice they get from advisors and authors is myopic, counterproductive, and in some cases, outright harmful.

The data support this thesis, and the trend is well known. For example, a ninety-year review tracking millions of individuals from 1850 to 1940 found that among the top 0.1 percent of wealth holders, 85 percent fell out of the category within a decade. Even among the broader top 1 percent, 72 percent fell out within just ten years.[1] The adage "from shirtsleeves to shirtsleeves in three generations" captures the prevailing sentiment that accumulated wealth is difficult to pass down to succeeding generations without squandering it.

There are all kinds of strategies and structures to mitigate this problem, but trusts and trainings frequently fall short because too many families focus on protecting their financial capital while failing to invest in their human capital. A child unprepared for abundance will either waste it or waste away because of it—or both. Harvard's Human Flourishing Index reveals what is plainly evident with too many wealthy families—that there exists a negative correlation between wealth and well-being.[2] In a *New York Times* op-ed describing their research, the study's authors noted that no high-income nations ranked in the top half of countries whose residents feel happiness and purpose in their lives. "We need to figure out how to foster economic development without compromising meaning, purpose, and relationships," they wrote.[3]

Simply put, society is producing affluent families who are materially rich and emotionally impoverished. Yet the "solutions" offered to fix this problem often make it worse. Advisors talk endlessly about "next-gen engagement," "succession planning," and "family governance." But behind the polished language lies a simple truth: Most of these programs exist not to build *agency* but to protect *assets*. Their true goal is retention—keeping the family's money under management. If you look closely, you'll see the perverse incentive at work. These advisors need dependent heirs. They need clients who can't imagine life without them. But dependency is precisely what destroys capability. A system designed to preserve wealth often ends up producing heirs who can't preserve themselves. Families deserve better than that.

This challenge has been on our minds for our entire lives. I say *our* because this book is a joint collaboration between two people. But coauthoring a book is an odd thing; some readers assume that both people are hunched over a shared computer or collaborating on a document, perhaps taking turns on each chapter.

More often than not—and as is the case with this book—there's a sort of division of labor. I'm Connor, and I'm the one writing this book. I'll share my ideas and perspectives in the first person; Taylor, my coauthor, will be referenced in the third person. But the ideas presented are a melding of our complementary but very different perspectives on this topic.

I grew up surrounded by conversations about legacy, trusts, and the careful transfer of wealth. My mother, an estate-planning attorney, spent her working days helping families safeguard the fruits of a lifetime's labor. Yet most of the stories she shared with me were warnings about wealth;

over and over again, she witnessed her clients' offspring squander their inheritance and lead chaotic lives. Instead of building upon their parents' foundation, they were wearing it down.

Decades later, my career took me into a different world: one of ideas, entrepreneurship, and education. As founder of Libertas Network, I've spent my life helping people create wealth—through enterprise, innovation, and the discipline of value creation. I've written over fifty books, taught millions of kids about money and entrepreneurial mindset through the *Tuttle Twins*, helped hundreds of thousands of kids start a business through our Kids Markets program, and worked with countless wealth creators who built their own empires from scratch. I've seen both sides of wealth: the forging of it, and the corrosion it can cause when meaning is missing.

My mother's stories have stayed with me as I've helped new generations of builders create financially successful lives. But the question has remained: How do we build wealth without it corrupting our children?

This question is not abstract for Taylor, whose life offers a rare vantage point into this dilemma. As a fifth-generation member of an affluent family enterprise, he has witnessed both the power and the peril of multigenerational wealth firsthand. He grew up watching how inherited abundance shapes identity, expectations, and family dynamics; later, as a leader within his family office and an advisor to many others, he saw how easily well-intended structures can drift into dependency. Many of the frameworks and ideas I'll share later come from his unique insights, gained through his personal struggle with abundance while carving out a life of meaning and purpose.

Both Taylor and I are focused on helping our ultra-high-net-worth friends and clients tackle this topic to build immunity from the trends befalling so many other affluent families. I do that through our NextGen Builders project, which provides instructional materials and consulting services to help families and grandparents instill an entrepreneurial mindset in their children and grandchildren. Taylor creates value for the same families through Belief Partners, where he provides guidance on establishing family office and trust structures that will help, not hinder, subsequent generations. We'll share more about these programs in Appendix A.

Before diving into the book, I'll pose a question to you: Is money the real problem affluent families struggle with regarding their children, or is it their *focus* on money? Taylor and I contend that wealth is not evil; it's energy. It magnifies what already exists: our values, our habits, and our assumptions about purpose. Left untethered from meaning, that energy corrodes. This is the wealth trap. But when directed toward creation, it compounds. In the parable of the talents in the Bible, for example, the faithful steward is rewarded not for caution, but for creation. He takes what he's given and multiplies its value. That's the divine pattern of progress: value creation through stewardship and service.

The same pattern applies to families. True wealth is not the accumulation of money, but the capacity to create value for others. Financial capital is simply the by-product of that deeper wealth—*human capital*. When families lose sight of this, the balance sheet may grow, but the spirit that produced those assets withers. Our challenge, then, is to pass on not only resources, but *resourcefulness*—to raise children who see wealth not as insulation from struggle, but as an invitation to build.

Most books about family wealth chase symptoms: entitlement, miscommunication, ungrateful heirs. These are real problems, but they are not root problems. They are the predictable by-products of something deeper: the loss of purpose, identity, and responsibility. You can't lecture your children into gratitude, or design a trust clause that promotes entrepreneurial thinking. Meaning doesn't trickle down through documents. It's transmitted through example, conversation, and culture. Legacy is not what you leave—it's *who you leave*. And no amount of financial capital can compensate for a deficit of human capital. That's why this book won't tell you how to protect your money. It will show you how to protect your *meaning*.

Taylor and I have seen the same pattern repeat across generations and industries: The families who endure are the ones who build a culture of creation. They raise *builders, not beneficiaries*—children who understand that meaning is not inherited, but earned through contribution. We've written this for the family that's already achieved success but feels the weight of it. For the patriarch or matriarch who lies awake, wondering if prosperity will dull their children's drive. For the grandparent who worries that the next generation won't understand what it took to get here—or what it takes to stay free. Our message is simple but demanding: Prosperity must serve purpose, or it becomes poison. And while this book is written to help affluent families avoid the wealth trap, the principles apply to families across the socioeconomic spectrum. Whether you steward millions or simply aspire to one day do so, the task is the same: Clarify your purpose, build systems of meaning, and raise builders who create more value than they consume.

Each chapter of this book will offer two principles, two frameworks, and a practical application. This structure moves from philosophy to practice—from ideas to action. We'll explore how meaning is built, how family culture is transmitted, and how to design systems that keep freedom alive. You'll see how to move from preservation to creation, from wealth as insulation to wealth as invitation. You'll learn to build a family operating system—a living framework that compounds capability, character, and contribution across generations. Our goal isn't to make you feel guilty for your success. It's to show you how to redeem it.

If you've ever felt that quiet fear—*Will success ruin my children?*—this book is for you. The truth is, it doesn't have to. Abundance can strengthen character instead of softening it. Wealth can expand purpose rather than erode it. But that outcome isn't automatic; it's engineered through culture, clarity, and conviction. This is your opportunity to reframe what your wealth means—for you, your children, and the generations that will follow. The task before us is both ancient and urgent: to build not only fortunes, but *families of builders.*

Introduction

"I've never really had to work for what I want," one of our interviewees shared with me. We'll call him Jacob, as he asked to remain anonymous, in part due to his personal embarrassment over his situation. "I'm now thirty-two years old and only recently started working, because spending my days doing basically nothing became quite boring. I'm a man-child, and I'm not happy about it," he said. When asked what his relationship to his inherited wealth was like, Jacob was direct: "The fear of losing what my parents worked so hard to build is all-consuming. I feel like I need to protect what they gave me."

Most successful parents want their children to build on what they've created—but most don't. You work for decades to create opportunity, only to discover that opportunity alone does not create capability. In theory, each generation (like Jacob's) should begin life at a higher rung than the one before it. They should inherit not merely wealth, but wisdom; not simply comfort, but the conditions to surpass those who came before them. With more access to knowledge, technology, mentors, and resources than in any previous era, the compounding of human capital should be inevitable. Human capital—the inner engine of capability, character, and creativity—is the only capital that reliably grows across generations (when cultivated with intention, of course). It is the foundation of every enduring fortune, and when it compounds, it produces outcomes no balance sheet can replicate.

And yet, across time and across cultures, the opposite happens with painful predictability. The first generation is characterized by value creation by someone who is hungry, driven, and disciplined by necessity. The second becomes the steward of the resulting resources—like Jacob, grateful for the opportunity they inherited and determined to protect it, but one step removed from the struggle that forged it. By the third generation, that distance becomes a chasm. Value creation gives way to value consumption. Comfort replaces hunger. Identity detaches from effort. The habits that built the prosperity are forgotten, and the responsibility that accompanics abundance feels foreign, even burdensome. Creation turns into preservation, preservation drifts into consumption, and consumption inevitably collapses into decay. This is the wealth trap in its most predictable form. The generational arc that should bend upward flattens and then begins its slow decline.

Families often respond to this pattern by tightening control—more rules, more oversight, more structures designed to "protect" the wealth. But as we'll explore in chapter 5, focusing on preservation is precisely what accelerates decline! When parents focus obsessively on protecting financial capital, it is usually because their human capital is already thinning. The deterioration of wealth is not the cause of family decline—it is the symptom. The root issue is the erosion of identity, purpose, agency, and meaning. Once those begin to fade, wealth becomes an accelerant of fragility rather than a force for flourishing. This is the sad trend that *The Wealth Trap* was written to fix.

Taylor's childhood offers a striking counterexample to the fragility observed in many affluent families. When he was in middle school, his family purchased an automotive manufacturing company that produced superchargers for high-performance cars. Suddenly, their world was full of engines, race cars, and possibilities. One night at dinner, fueled by adolescent excitement, he told his father, "We should advertise on the radio. Everyone should know about these superchargers!" It was the kind of naive idea most parents would brush aside with a gentle explanation of why things don't work that way. But his father didn't correct him. He simply said, "All right. Go do it."

Thirteen-year-old Taylor—armed with nothing but curiosity—called a major Los Angeles radio station, scheduled a meeting, and produced a commercial. Two weeks later, riding the school bus, he heard his own ad play over the airwaves. In that moment, something irreversible happened. He realized he could act on an idea and bring it to life. The world was not a fixed structure to be navigated cautiously; it was a malleable environment he could shape. The experience sparked confidence, yes—but it also launched an identity. Years later, his brother would toast him at his wedding by saying, "Taylor isn't bound by rules about what he can or can't do. If he decides to build something, he just starts." You can just *do* things has become Taylor's default approach to tackling challenges or seeing opportunities. His meaning is his agency is his purpose: to be a builder and solve problems through value creation.

This simple act of parental empowerment—a father's small invitation to take initiative—became the seed of a builder mindset. It taught Taylor that agency grows through action, not instruction; through experimentation, not explanation. That one experience set off a cascade of subsequent ventures, risks, and creations. (And failures!) It revealed the truth at the heart of this book: When wealth is paired with meaning and initiative, it becomes fuel. When it is paired with protectionism and caution, it quietly becomes a cage.

Our first chapter will examine how wealth amplifies values, for better or worse. This magnification effect means that a family's purpose—discussed in chapter 6—determines whether abundance elevates or erodes these values. Money magnifies clarity or confusion, virtue or vice, purpose or purposelessness. Left without meaning, wealth can be a chain that quietly enslaves—the wealth trap at its most insidious; rooted in meaning, it becomes wings that expand freedom and purpose. A child unprepared for abundance will either squander it or be suffocated by it. A child strengthened by purpose will transform abundance into fuel. *Identity is built, not bought.* It is forged through contribution, responsibility, and creative struggle. When families fail to intentionally cultivate meaning, money becomes a burden that subsidizes mediocrity rather than catalyzing greatness.

This dynamic applies both to families and the aggregate thereof—entire civilizations. Human progress, of course, is an outgrowth of family progress. The hockey-stick trajectory of wealth that propelled societies upward through innovation, prosperity, and flourishing (see figure 1) is not guaranteed.[1] It emerges only when individuals pursue purpose. When meaning erodes, decline follows. The Roman Empire, for example, collapsed not because it lacked wealth, but because it lost the virtues and vision that produced that wealth in the first place; it was, as the eighteenth-century historian Edward Gibbon wrote, "the natural and inevitable effect of immoderate greatness."[2] Comfort displaced contribution. Luxury replaced labor. Identity ceased to be forged through effort, and the culture inverted from value creation to value consumption.[3]

Humans are not wired for unbroken comfort. As odd as it sounds, we have an innate allergy to prosperity. We require struggle—not misery, but constructive struggle—in pursuit of something meaningful. Viktor Frankl saw this truth with brutal clarity during his imprisonment in Auschwitz. As he watched fellow prisoners endure deprivation far beyond what most humans will ever face, he noticed a striking pattern: Those who anchored themselves to a purpose—something still worth living for—possessed a strength that defied their circumstances. They survived not because their conditions improved, but because their meaning did. Frankl summarized it powerfully through Nietzsche's words: "He who has a *why* to live for can bear almost any *how*."[4] His insight was simple but profound: Meaning does not erase struggle, but it transforms it; it gives the human spirit something to push against and something to move toward. This *why* strengthens individuals—and this same *why* is what affluent families must cultivate if they hope to raise children capable of thriving amid abundance rather than crumbling under it.

THE HOCKEY STICK OF HUMAN PROGRESS

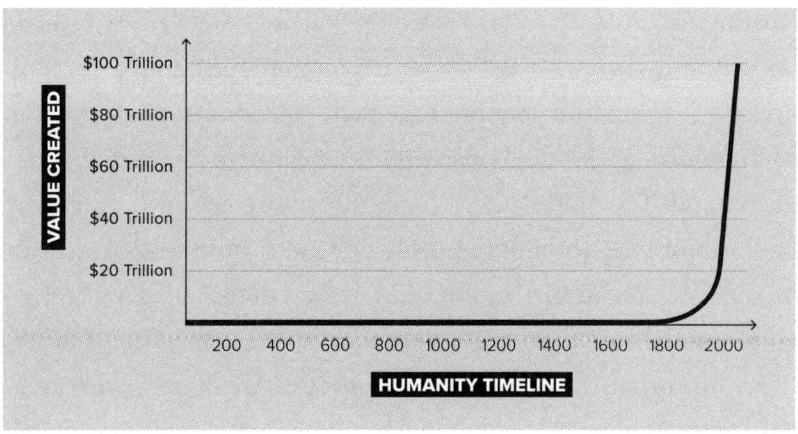

Figure 1

Without meaning, abundance corrodes. With meaning, abundance compounds. This is why self-actualization, or the active development of your gifts and passions to best create value for others in ways that are meaningful to you, must sit at the center of any multigenerational strategy. Self-actualization is not a luxury for the fortunate; it is the engine of human growth, whether in societal hockey sticks or in your own small family. After all, a family cannot thrive on financial capital alone; it thrives only with healthy human capital—individuals each pursuing who they can best become. And because families are relational ecosystems, not isolated individuals, self-actualization spreads. It elevates others, sets new norms, and raises the ceiling for everyone. Self-actualization can be contagious.

Without intentional effort to cultivate human capital, self-actualization gives way to self-destruction. Take Brandon Johnson, whose grandfather exemplified the classic first-generation builder—transforming a $5,000 loan in the 1940s into Katy Industries, a conglomerate with forty-three subsidiaries at its peak. Despite establishing a single-family office in 1971 and amassing substantial wealth, he neglected the human capital component and had no succession plan. Not trusting his children to take over, the business was left to a son-in-law—Brandon's father—which led his mom to file for divorce, family litigation, and permanent estrangement so complete that when one of Brandon's uncles died, many family members didn't even attend his funeral. The grandfather's financial empire became a cautionary tale—proof that, without the deliberate cultivation of character and capability, generational wealth transfer can, in fact, be devastating.

We've all heard that hard times create strong men who create good times, and that those good times produce weak men who create hard times. This cycle seems true, but is neither law nor fate; it is the predictable consequence of prosperity divorced from meaning. Strong men don't have to create "good times" that soften their descendants. They can create *meaningful* times. They can transform comfort into responsibility, wealth into valued work, and abundance into purposeful struggle. Prosperity without purpose produces weakness. Prosperity in the service of contribution produces strength.

This may be a lot to absorb as you reflect on your own family. Your children—and your grandchildren, if you have them—each develop their own personalities, convictions, and experiences that shape how they think about money and meaning. They have agency and form their own identities. Trying to align multiple individuals, each with distinct lives and motivations, can feel like herding cats. The way through this complexity is to lengthen your time horizon. Approaching this challenge with only one or two generations in mind is insufficient. If you want to break the shirtsleeves-to-shirtsleeves cycle, you cannot think in years or decades; you must think, audacious as it sounds, in centuries. Think ten generations ahead. Or better yet, think perpetually. Ask yourself: What culture are we building today that will increase the likelihood that our remote descendants—posterity we will never meet—will have the freedom, agency, and capacity to pursue their own self-actualization? The moment you force yourself to see beyond the next birthday, the next school year, or the next inheritance event, everything shifts. You stop asking, "How do I protect what I built?" and instead ask, "How do I empower others to continue building?"

Famed entrepreneur coach Dan Sullivan has long understood the power of improving your current circumstances by enlarging your vision of the future—in this case, considering your multigenerational descendants. "The only way to make your present better," Dan says, "is by making your future bigger."[5] A long horizon disciplines short-term decision-making, elevating expectations and exposing whether you are transmitting wealth or transmitting capability. Forecasting for the future reveals the need for a family operating system (which we'll discuss in chapter 8)—not a loose collection of values or sporadic conversations, but a deliberate, living architecture through which identity, purpose, and human capital are cultivated and passed down.

The world your descendants will inherit is unlike anything previous generations have faced. It will be radically different even from your own experience. Artificial intelligence, robotics, and automation will erase predictable career paths and dissolve entire categories of work. The ladder you climbed will likely not be available for them. Their path will not be linear, conventional, or guaranteed. In this emerging world, the most essential skill is not mastery of existing systems, but the ability to create value in unknown environments.

Rules are inadequate for such a world, including rules around work and wealth transfer. Rules assume stable conditions and predictable outcomes. They teach compliance, not creativity. They prepare children for yesterday, not tomorrow. And when the world shifts—as it always does—rules easily shatter. As Mike Tyson famously put it, "Everybody has plans until they get hit."[6] Families built on plans collapse under the first punch. But families built on frameworks adapt. Frameworks teach judgment. They help a child understand how to navigate the unfamiliar, not merely how to perform the familiar. They are portable, flexible, and timeless. They teach a child *how* to think, not *what* to think. And this is precisely what the next generation will need: adaptive intelligence anchored in enduring principles.

Consultants often prescribe rigid processes—family governance protocols, forced meeting structures, scripted communication systems. These are rules disguised as wisdom, and they produce form without much substance. They do not cultivate agency but instead manufacture dependence. Rigid processes offer the illusion of control while quietly eroding capability. But frameworks are different. Frameworks empower. They invite participation and share concepts with multiple layers of application and meaning for one's particular circumstances. They grow with the child and prepare families to face a world in which change is constant and meaning must be cultivated rather than inherited.

At the center of all of this is the dramatic distinction between builders and beneficiaries. Builders turn wealth into capability; beneficiaries turn it into comfort. Builders see abundance as raw material for creation; beneficiaries see it as insulation from responsibility. Builders start from strength—standing on the shoulders of giants—and then build the next rungs on the ladder. Beneficiaries inherit the ladder but never climb it. They confuse assets with identity, and comfort with purpose. But a family whose children do not climb eventually collapses under its own weight. Self-actualization gives way to self-destruction.

Each generation should begin from strength, not from scratch. But strength must be measured the right way—not in financial assets but in human capital, such as skills, resilience, effort, empathy, creativity, courage, and value creation. Financial capital is simply the by-product of human capital. When families forget this, they nourish the symptoms of success while starving the sources of it. Wealth should be understood as a means of human flourishing—of deepening identity, strengthening relationships, and expanding contribution. Wealth exists to expand freedom. But freedom without responsibility erodes character, and the absence of responsibility turns privilege into poison.

This is why wealth's purpose is not preservation—it's progression. Preservation is defensive. Progression is generative. Preservation clings to what was built; progression builds what comes next. The only inheritance that truly endures is the capacity to build. John Adams captured this truth when he urged his wife to "fire [our children] with ambition to be useful."[7] Not comfortable. Not entitled. *Useful.* That is the heartbeat of capability, the essence of human capital. That is the antidote to the shirtsleeves-to-shirtsleeves cycle.

When families raise builders instead of beneficiaries, wealth becomes a force for flourishing rather than fragility. Builders do not drift; they design. They create meaning rather than waiting for it. They contribute to the world instead of simply consume it. They are equipped for both prosperity and adversity—strong enough to withstand volatility, disciplined enough to pursue meaningful work, responsible enough to transform freedom into purpose. And in a world defined by uncertainty, builders are the ones who will thrive.

This book will show you how to cultivate these builders. It will guide you in constructing a family operating system that transmits identity, purpose, responsibility, and agency across generations. You will be equipped with frameworks—rooted in psychology, philosophy, behavioral economics, and lived experience—that prepare your posterity for a future where adaptability, creativity, and contribution matter more than credentials or compliance. This book will help you reorient your wealth toward meaning, so your children inherit not just comfort but capability.

If you embrace this task, you will create a family where abundance strengthens rather than weakens, where prosperity amplifies purpose rather than eroding it, and where each generation begins not merely with more resources but with more resourcefulness. You will build a lineage not of consumers, but of creators. You will raise human capital who understand that financial capital is not the end but the means—the energy that enables them to build, to serve, and to rise.

The work ahead is demanding, but it is necessary to build your legacy. It asks you to think beyond your own lifetime and to act beyond your own comfort, to reframe what it means to succeed and to rediscover the purpose of prosperity. You will be asked to choose meaning over ease and contribution over consumption. And if you do, you will give your children—and their children—a gift far greater than money. You will give them the meaning and capacity to build.

CHAPTER 1

The Paradox of Prosperity

Claiborne Haw never expected prosperity to create a crisis. She had grown up around comfort, attended excellent schools, built a respectable professional path, and learned to operate competently within the structures of traditional success. When her grandparents passed away and she received a windfall inheritance—as a fourth-generation inheritor related to Luck Companies, a one-hundred-year-old stone business—Claiborne stepped out of her corporate role and into a rare freedom that most people imagine as the pinnacle of ease. She no longer needed to work for money. The gift felt liberating—at least, at first.

The initial weeks of her sabbatical felt expansive: unstructured days, slow mornings, travel, leisure, flexibility. But before long the freedom revealed a darker contour. Possibility without direction began to erode her sense of momentum. Days blended together and decisions felt weightless. She described it as drifting through "limitless options that all felt the same." Eventually the disorientation hardened into something more troubling. "If this is all there is, it's not enough," she told us.[1] In her words, Claiborne felt she was "perishing for lack of vision"[2]—she had lifted the burden of obligation, yet found herself losing a deeper structure she didn't know she needed.

Few affluent families see this dynamic clearly until it manifests in one of their own children or grandchildren. The problem is not the presence of resources but the absence of direction. When the pressure to survive disappears, so does the natural behavioral scaffolding that once forced people to grow. Hardship teaches resourcefulness; prosperity typically shields people from ever needing to develop it. Claiborne's twenty-two-month sabbatical was more than simply the product of privilege. It was the predictable outcome of abundance without intention.

Comfort, left unexamined, corrodes. Prosperity is pleasant, even helpful—but it is never neutral. It dissolves the very constraints that often shape identity and build capability. When you remove necessity, you remove the conditions under which people most intuitively discover meaning. And unless families intentionally replace those conditions with something better, comfort becomes a sedative. Problems that once demanded engagement now disappear with a phone call, an advisor, or a distribution. Parents understandably want to minimize their children's suffering, but in doing so, they unintentionally minimize their children's growth. Wealth cannot shield people from this psychological law: Human beings develop through effort, responsibility, and contribution—not through insulation.

This dynamic does not always reveal itself with existential questions or with great fanfare. Sometimes it shows up in the smallest, most ordinary moments. During Taylor's teen years, for example, his family's automotive company overflowed with beautiful test vehicles. At age sixteen, he was asked what kind of first car he wanted. Why not one of the dozens of amazing vehicles sitting in the shop? His parents agreed, and for years, he drove a rotation of American show cars, swapping every few months for something new. (This was during his phase of being, in his own words, "an entitled little shit.")

His lifestyle was thrilling. But it also taught an unspoken lesson neither he nor his parents recognized at the time. Taylor never had a car long enough to consider what was required to maintain it. He never changed the oil, checked tire wear, or noticed early signs of mechanical stress. The cars weren't his; they were temporary toys. When one was returned to the shop with a damaged engine, Taylor was startled at how embarrassed he felt. Since he wasn't required to take care of it, he never did. Only later did he understand how formative that small experience had been. Without responsibility, he did not develop capability. The structure around him removed the need to care, and so caring never formed.

Parents often believe that insulation is kindness, just as Taylor's father believed he was being generous. But generosity that removes all consequence is not empowerment, but the opposite: erosion. Prosperous families unintentionally create worlds so comfortable, so buffered, that responsibility itself begins to feel optional. In these environments, young people rarely confront the productive discomfort where meaning is naturally forged: the need to solve problems, endure consequences, or persevere in uncertainty. The absence of necessity creates a lack of growth. And in that vacuum, identity atrophies.

When comfort starts to hollow out the next generation, most families don't recognize it as a meaning problem; they interpret it as a behavior problem. They notice missed opportunities, half-hearted efforts, worrying choices, and what appears to be entitlement, and conclude that the answer must be tighter structure. So they redesign the trust documents, formalize family councils, create investment committees, add approval layers, implement next-gen programs, and build governance that feels more like a firewall than a framework. On the surface, the structure looks responsible, even sophisticated. Underneath, it sometimes sends a quiet message: We don't trust you with freedom. Worried that the next generation will squander their inheritance, parents often try to fastidiously preserve the wealth they fear will destroy their kids.

Preservation Undermines Prosperity

In our work with families, we encounter this reflex to build more structure so often that Taylor began describing it as the "Four Horsemen of Destruction": preservation, protectionism, stewardship, and collectivism. Each one sounds noble on the surface but is rooted in real fears. And each one, if left unaddressed, tends to accelerate the very outcomes the family is trying to prevent.

Preservation is the first horseman. Once wealth has been created, the goal quietly shifts from value creation to wealth preservation. The systems and strategies implemented, often in the form of a "family office," tend to prioritize financial capital over human capital. This shift in strategy creates several subtle challenges. First, it establishes wealth as the primary concern. Second, it removes the need for active value creation, because preservation is almost always a passive strategy. Third, the family will tend to grow faster than the wealth will compound, so on a per-capita basis, wealth preservation simply doesn't work. Overall, preservation is in direct opposition to the entrepreneurial spirit that created the wealth in the first place—risk-taking, adaptation, creative destruction. When families retire that spirit and make preservation the primary objective, they embrace a self-defeating prophecy. The only sustainable way to carry a legacy forward is to keep re-creating it, treating each generation as a potential first-generation builder in their own right. More on this later.

Protectionism is the second horseman. Having seen what wealth can do to people, families understandably want to protect their children from being poisoned by it. In an effort to "set them up for success," they manufacture opportunities, remove barriers, and create opaque ideals of success and achievement. But these approaches can backfire if done poorly. The reason is that too much protection removes the liberty to stumble. The logical conclusion for the next generation is that risk is dangerous, and failure is unacceptable. Instead of producing resilient, creative adults, protectionism produces anxious heirs who are terrified to experiment or venture into uncharted territories. Yet all genuine success—in business, in relationships, in any meaningful domain—is built on a long trail of small failures that were survived, learned from, and integrated. The more families try to protect their children from falling, the less those children ever learn how to stand.

The third horseman shows up in how families approach succession and stewardship. Stewardship is a beautiful concept; it is also a dangerous identity. Embracing a role as a steward can dim one's vision for something more and disincentivize the calling to create. When succession is framed primarily as "who will steward what we built?" the implicit expectation is that the chosen one must protect, defend, and preserve the past. Everyone else is left wondering what role, if any, is left for them. People will tolerate that for a while, but most human beings eventually want autonomy and the chance to build something of their own. When "good children" are those who dutifully carry forward an inherited script, they can easily lose sight of who they are capable of becoming while resenting the script that was written for them. In reality, every succession is a new founding moment. The healthiest families are those where the next generation is empowered to treat the legacy as raw material for new creation, not as a relic to be guarded. Taylor calls this "perpetual gen 1"—each generation supported in becoming a first-generation value creator in their own right, often building parallel ventures that eventually loop back and enrich the family as a whole. We'll discuss this in chapter 5.

The fourth horseman is collectivism—the tendency of enterprising families to build governance structures that prize harmony and control above all else. In the name of unity, they centralize decision-making, formalize elaborate councils, and create top-down bureaucracies that look strangely like the political systems that once opposed the very free-market dynamism that created the wealth. (And ironically, these collectivist structures formed to promote family unity paradoxically increase the likelihood that everyone ends up suing each other.) Control feels safer than influence. But control does not scale; it is limited by the bandwidth of those in charge and the boundaries of the governance structure. Influence, by contrast, can travel anywhere. When everything must run through the center, family members face a false choice: Either work inside the system on its terms, or leave entirely. A more life-giving approach decentralizes authority—allowing branches or nuclear families to operate as semiautonomous hubs connected to a shared infrastructure and story. That structure invites voluntary collaboration rather than forced collectivism, and it allows individuals to pursue self-actualization while still contributing to the larger legacy.

This preservation paradigm is a family system organized around preserving what was built, rather than empowering future generations to build. It feels prudent and often looks sophisticated. But underneath, it usually converts wealth from a source of energy into a set of restraints. The antidote is simply a return to the question that animated the original builder: What are we here to create, and how do we empower our descendants to continue creating?

Maslow's Sailboat

None of this becomes clear, however, until a family begins to ask more profound questions about the psychology of prosperity. Why does comfort undermine motivation? Why do those who have the most often feel the least internal drive? Why does a young adult like Claiborne—capable, intelligent, well-supported—experience disorientation when given the very freedom she was raised to expect?

Part of the answer lies in Maslow's famous hierarchy of needs, though not in the way most people think. Maslow's pyramid is well known: Humans must satisfy physiological and safety needs before they can pursue belonging, esteem, and self-actualization. In contexts of scarcity, the model may make sense.[3] But in affluent environments, physiological and safety needs are not just met—they are permanently solved. Children never confront the fear of hunger, the anxiety of instability, or the urgency of survival. They are born into a world where the lower layers of Maslow's pyramid are already achieved.

This means the traditional model breaks down. Survival is no longer the motivator. Safety is no longer the goal. Meaning becomes the central psychological driver instead. Without a clear hierarchy to traverse, the next generation must discover direction. They must learn who they are, what they can do, and what they find meaningful. These are higher-order questions that the pyramid model cannot adequately address.

A better metaphor for families to consider is a sailboat (see figure 2). The hull represents stability: food, safety, belonging. The sail represents purpose: esteem, self-actualization, and self-transcendence. Both are needed for the boat to sail. But here is the critical insight: A family can build an extraordinarily strong hull, but their children will still drift if the sails are not developed. An overbuilt hull produces comfort without motion. A tiny sail, lacking tension or direction, cannot catch wind. Put differently, focusing on financial capital (providing material resources and all their benefits) without investing in human capital will produce drifting descendants.

MASLOW'S SAILBOAT MODEL

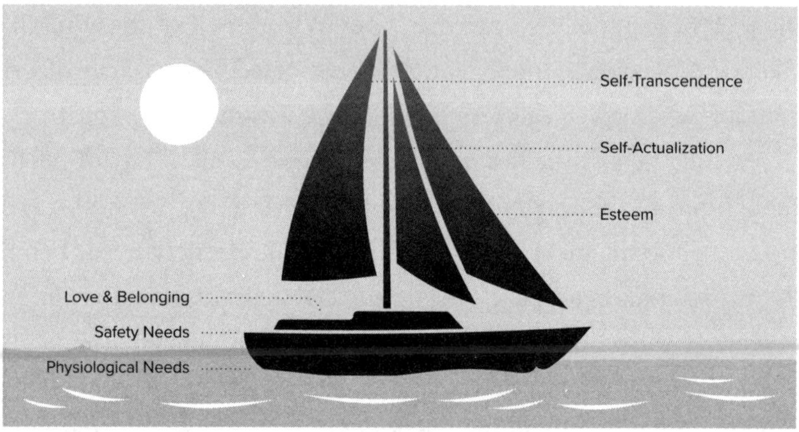

Figure 2

We might say that Claiborne had a beautifully constructed hull. She had belonging, safety, stability, relationships, and heritage. But her sail—her sense of direction and purpose—remained small because it had never been required to expand. Her life had always moved forward through structure, not vision. When the structure dissolved, nothing replaced it. The hull did its job; the sail could not.

Affluent children often grow up with these oversized hulls and undersized sails. Parents, striving to give their children the lives they never had, remove friction and replace it with abundance. The result is lives that feel secure but directionless, cushioned but unanchored. Tasks are handled by others, problems are outsourced, and schedules are managed. Consequences are softened or removed entirely. The child, swimming in stability, receives few opportunities to exercise agency, responsibility, or initiative.

The consequences of this imbalance may unfold slowly, but they are profound. Without opportunities to engage reality, children never build conviction. Without responsibility, they never build resilience. Without necessity, they never build identity. Prosperity thus becomes a quiet architect of drift. Wealth, although not inherently harmful, removes the discomfort that once compelled movement.

None of this is the fault of wealth itself. Prosperity can be a tremendous blessing, unlocking opportunities that were unimaginable just a generation earlier. Wealth can provide stability, safety, education, experiences, and, perhaps most powerful of all, time. But when prosperity becomes untethered from meaning, it becomes a sedative. The antidote is not guilt or restrictions but *intention*. Wealth must be paired with purpose. Stability must be paired with direction. Comfort must be paired with contribution. Building the hull must be balanced with creating a larger sail to match.

Claiborne's journey began to shift once she started asking questions, gathering information, engaging her family's system, and building community with others on similar paths. (In other words, once she focused on enlarging her sails.) "I realized I was living as if I could do nothing or everything and it wouldn't matter," she told us. "But it did. I knew I couldn't stay there. I could either dig my heels in deeper or take one small step forward." Importantly, the step Claiborne took was not born from perfect clarity but from refusing to remain idle. She didn't discover meaning by thinking her way into it. She *acted* her way into it. Meaning is built through movement, not mere contemplation. Prosperity can support that movement, but it can never substitute for it.

Value Reflected Back

When families understand this paradox, they realize they must engage their children in the pursuit of purpose. They recognize that insulating their children from every hardship is not a gift but a deprivation.

They see that comfort must be governed by intention, or it will quietly govern them—and even more, as we'll explore in chapter 9, comfort must be tempered by designed struggle to ensure our children build resilience. Finally, these families realize that the hull cannot carry the family forward without a sail. And they begin to build accordingly.

Once families begin to recognize how prosperity dulls the internal mechanisms that once generated momentum, they can finally see the deeper question behind so many of their struggles: How do we cultivate meaning in a context that no longer requires it? Children in affluent families may never face the biological urgency that pushed previous generations forward. They will likely never need to ask how they will eat or where they will live. Their shelter, safety, and social belonging are inherited, not built. And when those foundations are not earned, they do not generate identity; they simply exist by default.

Meaning, by contrast, must be built, not inherited. And when children begin life with a large hull and a nearly nonexistent sail, the absence of meaning becomes its own kind of storm. Lack of motivation doesn't cause the drift, but having nothing compelling to move toward does. Their lives contain no friction, no obstacles they are required to overcome, and no feedback loops that tell them who they are becoming. Over time, the absence of meaning feels like malaise, then anxiety, then shame. They sense internally what their parents often fail to see externally: that prosperity is not the same thing as purpose. (And worse, that the former usually erodes the latter.)

The primary path to building meaning is to initiate action and create value for others. As that value is reflected back to us, identity, connection, and purpose are created. Even if our initial actions are clumsy or counterproductive, the feedback we receive helps us iterate quickly and identify better opportunities to pursue. Consider a common occurrence in wealthy families: an investment committee that serves as a proving ground for decision-making. Family members are often invited to bring forward opportunities—new ventures, philanthropic ideas, or business acquisitions—for the committee of fellow family members to evaluate collectively. In theory, this is a way to engage the next generation and to get them thinking strategically about resource allocation.

Almost always, one family member participates without contributing. They never bring opportunities forward, often because they don't know how or feel unqualified, inexperienced, or anxious about looking foolish. And in that discomfort, they begin to perform a different role entirely: They critique. They find reasons why something won't work. They poke holes and challenge others' ideas, not out of malice but out of a deeper insecurity. When people do not know how to participate in creation, their only remaining option is to obstruct. Because their environment does not reflect back to them that they have value, they flail and founder, creating chaos that family members misinterpret as rebelliousness or sabotage. In reality, they are starving for confirmation that they matter. When no value is reflected back to them, they do the only thing they know how to do to generate a reaction: They push against what others are building. The family experiences this as friction and resistance; the individual experiences it as the only way to be seen as relevant. What looks like opposition is often simply the desperation of someone who has never experienced their contribution being mirrored back as meaningful. Until families recognize this dynamic, they will continue to pathologize what is, at its core, a value-reflection problem: a capable person who has never been invited, equipped, or expected to create value, and therefore has never had the chance to see who they are in the mirrored reflections of their environment. Contribution creates confidence; lack of contribution creates friction. And in the space of that friction, relationships rupture.

The concept of a value reflection (see figure 3) is relatively simple. Imagine a child at the center of their environment, surrounded by family, friends, classmates, or colleagues. When they act—creating, trying, initiating, proposing, building—their environment reflects something back to them. Sometimes that reflection is positive, signifying that what they did mattered. Sometimes it is negative, indicating that they missed the mark. But either way, the reflection helps them understand something about themselves. And that understanding shapes their following action. Over time, those cycles of action and reflection build identity. The more value we create, the more we experience the reciprocal recognition of that value; we become a by-product of those whose lives we impact, whether positively or negatively.

VALUE REFLECTIONS

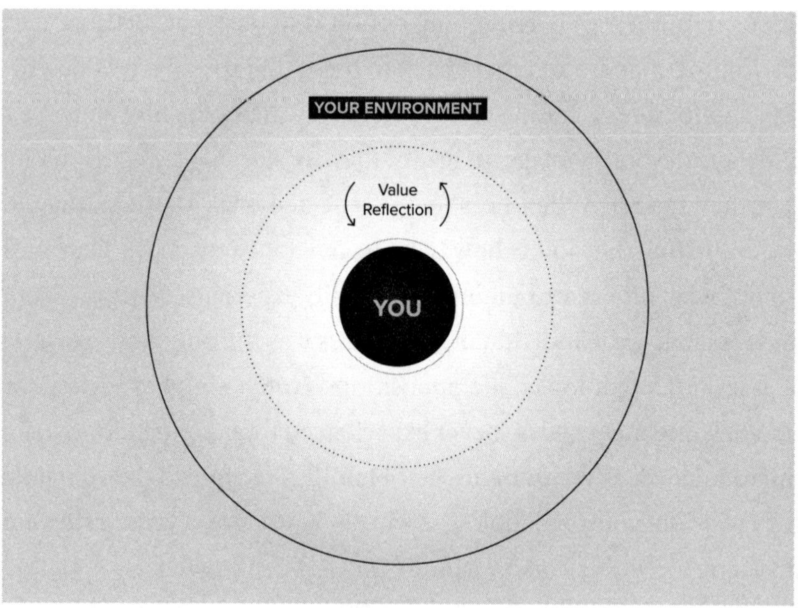

Figure 3

But when wealth removes the need for action, the cycle collapses. Children no longer engage in activities that generate reflection. Parents solve problems for them, institutions absorb consequences, and advisors manage processes. Wealth becomes a buffer, insulating them from the very experiences that would reveal who they are. And without sufficient reflection, identity remains unformed. An unformed identity is easily threatened. That is why so many affluent young people seem inexplicably anxious or defensive. They are not reacting to others but responding to the absence of a self. They feel oppressed by their environment because it does not reflect back that they exist or that their contributions have value. And it's easier to assume that feeling irrelevant is the environment's fault than acknowledging one's inability to make valuable contributions to one's environment. Humans have inherent value, but simply existing is not valuable in itself.

Creating Value for Others

Identity formed through value reflections is not something you can hand to a child with a lecture or a document. It has to be lived. Parents who understand this begin to pay much closer attention to the ecosystem they are creating around their children. Instead of asking only, "How do we protect them from bad outcomes?" they also ask, "Where do our children get to contribute? Where do they see that their effort matters?" The shift seems subtle, but it moves the focus from insulation to initiative, from shielding to shaping, from controlling to influencing.

One of the simplest ways to improve value reflections is to help children experience themselves as useful. Usefulness is underrated in affluent environments, where service can be outsourced at every turn. Yet usefulness is one of the primary ways human beings experience meaning. A child who cooks dinner for the family and sees everyone enjoy it experiences a value reflection. A teenager who helps a younger sibling master a skill experiences a value reflection. A grandchild who takes responsibility for organizing a small family gathering, and sees it go well, receives a powerful signal: I can make things happen. I can be of use.

Wealth can either dilute these experiences or amplify them. It dilutes them when parents use money to keep children from ever being needed. Wealth amplifies an experience when parents use money to support their children's efforts to be useful. Funding a child's business idea, for example, can be either corrosive or catalytic depending on the expectation attached. A check written to "keep them busy" sends one message; a far better message is sent if the funding is tied to a simple agreement: "You are responsible for building something that creates value for others, and we'll talk together about what you learn and how you grow." In one case, money is an anesthetic. In the other, it is fuel.

This is why purposeful wealth is so different from passive wealth. Passive wealth simply sits in preservation mode, waiting to be consumed. Purposeful wealth channels energy into building and contributing. It asks, over and over, not "What do we get?" but "What can we build and contribute?" That question alone begins to reshape a family culture. Parents who wake up asking it, and whose children hear them regularly wrestling with it, are teaching something far more potent than any formal lesson. They are demonstrating that prosperity is a starting line, not a finish line. They are showing that while the ship is sturdy, its sail still needs work.

Children, after all, tend to copy what they see, not what they hear. In families where parents continue to build—whether through businesses, philanthropy, teaching, art, caregiving, or community leadership—children absorb a particular pattern: When you have resources, you use them to create value. In families where parents primarily consume or simply steward existing structures, children absorb a different pattern: When you have resources, you protect them and enjoy them. Both groups of children may inherit similar balance sheets. They do not inherit similar scripts.

Some of the most resilient families we've seen have a quiet, almost unspoken bias toward service. Service might look like running a business that treats employees exceptionally well, or showing up for neighbors in crisis, or serving in a local church, or mentoring younger entrepreneurs. It might look like hosting people to create community or funding community projects to bring neighbors together. The form matters far less than the direction: energy flowing outward rather than inward. In such families, children grow up seeing that the point of prosperity is not to withdraw from the world, but to engage it more deeply.

Parents do not need to be perfect exemplars to create this culture. They only need to be honest strivers. It's powerful, for instance, when a parent can say to a teenager, "I'm still figuring out what I'm called to build next. Here's what I'm exploring. Here's what's hard about it. Here's what excites me." That kind of transparency does more to normalize trial and error than any prepackaged "career path" talk. It shows children that meaning is something adults continue to pursue, not something that was solved once and for all decades ago.

Expanding What Value Really Means

Parents can also help by broadening the definition of what constitutes a contribution. In preservation-oriented families, value is often measured in narrow, financial terms: deals done, assets grown, costs saved. But some of the most important contributions to the family's long-term flourishing—to its human capital, in particular—are invisible to spreadsheets. The sibling who holds relationships together. The cousin who quietly cares for aging grandparents. The aunt who serves in the community, building a reputation that influences how the family is treated. If these forms of value go unrecognized, those who provide them will understandably feel unseen, having received no reflection. If they are recognized and honored, children will learn that the family's definition of success includes a wide range of meaningful roles.

Ultimately, what parents are designing—whether consciously or not—is an operating system (which we'll explore in depth in chapter 8). They are establishing, through repeated choices, what their family is about. Is this a family where wealth exists primarily to preserve a lifestyle, or a family where wealth exists to support lives of contribution? Is this a family where comfort is treated as the end goal, or where comfort is treated as a starting point for deeper responsibility? Is this a family where the next generation is primarily evaluated on how well they protect the past, or on how courageously they build the future?

Children will answer these questions for themselves by watching their parents. They will internalize where their parents spend time, how they respond to problems, what they celebrate, and what they ignore. Over time, those patterns will become the stories they tell themselves about who they are. If those stories are rich in value reflections, rooted in contribution, and animated by creation rather than preservation, wealth will have been harnessed to something worthy. If those stories are thin, defensive, and consumption focused, no amount of governance can save the family from slow decay.

The paradox of prosperity will always be with us: The more comfortable life becomes, the less external pressure there is to grow. That is not something to lament but to recognize and design around. Families who understand this do not apologize for their success, nor do they idolize it. They simply refuse to let comfort be the main character in their story. They take seriously the work of building both the hull and the sail, of pairing stability with meaning, and of ensuring that their children experience themselves as creators of value, not merely consumers of it.

When that happens, prosperity ceases to be a sedative and becomes a stimulant. It stops eroding purpose and starts amplifying it. The wealth that could have dulled a generation instead deepens their impact. That is the possibility hidden inside every affluent family, if they are willing to see comfort as a force that must be governed—not the force that governs them. The point isn't to demonize comfort or celebrate suffering, but to discover callings worth suffering for. When we are compelled to pursue a life of deep meaning, rooted in a vision of who we can become, suffering becomes joyful.

Principles

1. **Abundance breeds apathy when meaning is not designed.** When prosperity removes necessity, it also removes the natural forces that build character, identity, and grit. In affluent families, children can live comfortably without ever needing to solve real problems or be genuinely useful—and in that vacuum, drift, numbness, and quiet despair set in. Unless parents intentionally create opportunities for contribution, responsibility, and purpose, comfort becomes a sedative that slowly hollows out their children.

2. **Wealth magnifies what already exists—values, vices, and vision.** Money doesn't change who a person is; it amplifies whatever is already there. In a family culture grounded in service, creation, and responsibility, wealth becomes fuel for outsized impact—but in a culture of fear, preservation, and consumption, the same wealth accelerates fragility and conflict. That's why the real work is not arranging the assets, but shaping the values and vision they will magnify.

Application Examples

These ideas matter most when translated from concept to concrete action. Below is a sampling of age-appropriate prompts to guide you with your children or grandchildren.

Get the full list at WealthTrapBook.com/list.

- **Ages 5–8**
  Give your child a rotating "job" that genuinely helps the family—setting the table, matching socks, feeding a pet, wiping the table after dinner. Make sure someone explicitly thanks them and names the impact. For example: "Because you fed the dog, we could finish cooking. That really helped." This builds the association: *I matter because I contribute, not just because I exist.*

- **Ages 9–12**
  Help them start a tiny venture: lemonade stand, handmade crafts, pet-walking, or a kid-run snack booth at a sports league. Let them choose, price, and sell. Debrief with them afterward: *What worked? What didn't? Who did we serve?* Be sure to emphasize learning and service, not profit.

- **Ages 13–17**
  Identify a small, real problem at school, in sports, at church, or in the community—and challenge them to design a solution. Examples: organizing a study group to help struggling students, improving a process on the sports team, or designing a better sign-up system for the nonprofit the family supports. Offer support, but let them experience obstacles, people saying no, and things not working perfectly.

- **Ages 18–25**
  Sit down together and map out where they currently experience meaning: work, relationships, creativity, faith, causes.

Ask them: “Where do you feel most alive?” or “Where do you feel invisible?” Then help them design one or two concrete actions in their highest-meaning areas that will generate value reflections (e.g., leading a small group, launching a project, mentoring younger students).

CHAPTER 2

Agency in an Institutional Age

When Huguette Clark died in 2011 at the age of 104, the newspapers mostly ran with the same image: a tiny, elegant woman in a fur-collared coat, photographed in the 1940s, looking somewhere just past the camera. What the photographs could not show were the rooms she left behind.

There was the 121-room mansion on Fifth Avenue where she grew up, the largest private residence in New York City at the time. There were the forty rooms she later owned in a different Fifth Avenue building, overlooking Central Park. There was the 21,000-square-foot estate in Santa Barbara facing the Pacific, and the fifty-two-acre property in New Canaan, Connecticut, with a formal name and a caretaker who worked there for twenty years without ever seeing his employer. All of them were empty. None of the rooms had seen parties, children or grandchildren tumbling down the halls, or family holidays. The staff trimmed hedges and dusted furniture in houses the owner had not visited in decades.

Huguette chose a different setting. After a doctor found her in her apartment in 1991, underweight, wrapped in a dirty bathrobe, with untreated skin cancer on her face, she was admitted to Beth Israel Medical Center in Manhattan. The treatment worked, and the cancer cleared. She could have returned to any of her homes, but she chose to stay in the hospital instead.

She paid hundreds of thousands of dollars a year for a standard two-bed room with the curtains drawn. She gave a false name to the staff to preserve her privacy. Most days, she walked slow circles around the room with her nurse and called it "walking around Central Park."[1] That small rectangle of floor became the whole of her physical world for the last twenty years of her life. But this was not merely a late-in-life seclusion; after a short-lived, childless marriage at age twenty-two, Huguette had lived with her mother for decades until her mother's 1963 death, after which Huguette withdrew almost entirely from society.

From that hospital bed, she dealt with the outside world as her reduced life required. She phoned lawyers, property managers, and staff at her estates to check on repairs and landscaping. She followed newspaper coverage of the stock market and local politics. And she sent instructions to an employee in Brooklyn whose full-time job was to maintain, dress, and photograph her dolls.

The dolls were not toys in the usual sense. She owned more than a thousand of them, along with elaborate houses and theaters built to her specifications. She ordered miniature custom outfits from French fashion houses and spent large sums at auctions on rare antique figures. She commissioned a Bavarian artist to paint scenes from fairy tales on tiny house walls and argued over whether the fronts should be fifteen or nineteen inches wide. She hired a Japanese artist to visit temples and castles and produce scale drawings so that the costumes and architecture in her kabuki models would be historically correct down to the smallest detail. When a craftsman built a ceiling too low, she sent word that "the little people are banging their heads" and asked him to raise it.[2]

Her energy went into that world—not into building a household of her own, raising children, or starting schools or hospitals or ventures that would outlive her in any tangible human sense. She was generous with people who came into her orbit, but almost all of those relationships were transactional and single-sided. The people closest to her were employees. The people related to her by blood were kept at arm's length or shut out entirely.

This is not a morality tale about an eccentric old woman. It is, however, a stark picture of what can happen when wealth allows someone to let institutions and staff do almost all of the work of living. Huguette was not helpless or senile for most of her time in the hospital, let alone the decades of seclusion she spent prior. Those who spoke with her regularly said she was sharp, funny, and remarkably knowledgeable about history and art. She simply preferred a world where she could control information and minimize direct human contact. Her money made that preference sustainable. No doubt it also made her life easy.

Huguette represents one end of a spectrum. Few families will ever have the means, or the inclination, to live in isolation while hired help takes care of literally everything. But many will feel a gentler pull in the same direction. When you have enough capital, allowing systems and professionals to run your life is remarkably easy. If you are not careful, you can wake up one day and discover that you own a great deal on paper but control almost nothing in practice.

The Rise of the Systems

For most children in developed countries, life from age five onward is shaped by institutions. School determines where they sit, when they speak, what they work on, and when they can use the bathroom. Day-care staff look after them after school. Coaches run heavily regulated youth sports leagues. Therapists help smooth out their rough edges. Entertainment is outsourced to dopamine-driven digital apps. DoorDash delivers dinner.

Families of means add a further layer. Their kids have private schools, college consultants, travel planners, tutors, personal assistants, lawyers, accountants, and wealth managers. Each institution, standing alone, fills a legitimate niche. Together, they can create a life where almost every significant decision is mediated by a professional or a platform. The family does not so much choose as consent.

Institutions serve a purpose but are in constant tension with personal agency. As figure 4 shows, when reliance on outside help is very low, families bear a greater burden by exerting their agency to be directly involved in decision-making and subsequent action. They might educate their children at home, cook meals together (using food from their homestead), design family activities, fix their own appliances (with help from YouTube!), or organize neighborhood sports leagues or community programs. Agency is high. So is the burden. In a complex world, this posture can become its own kind of trap.

Move a bit to the right, and a healthier balance appears. The family uses institutions as tools. Children attend school or various classes, but parents remain involved in what they are learning. A tax professional helps with filings, but the parents still understand enough to ask questions. An investment advisor manages a portion of the portfolio, but the family is deeply involved and informed. The family eats out a few times a week, but focuses on cooking a delicious Sunday meal to enjoy together and keep the tradition alive. Agency dips from its peak but stabilizes at a level that leaves the family in charge. This is what we might call the sweet spot—reliance on institutions that save time and augment capacity without significantly surrendering judgment or diminishing agency.

INSTITUTIONALIZATION VS. AUTONOMY

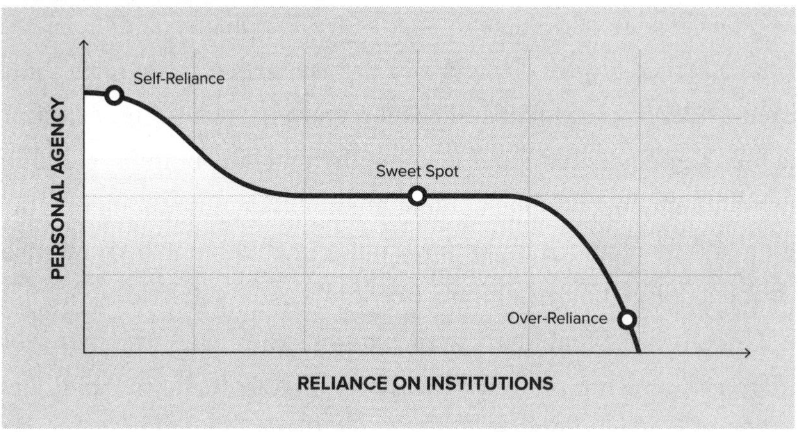

Figure 4

Slide further right and the curve plummets. The family leans heavily on systems and staff. They treat school as the primary place for moral or social formation, not just academic training. They treat doctors, counselors, and coaches—the "experts"—as the final word on matters once discussed at the dinner table. They treat lawyers, accountants, and family offices as the only people capable of understanding the structures that now hold their wealth. Agency falls. At the far right, it hits zero. The family has become a client in every domain. That final state feels organized. Bills are paid automatically. Children are "on track." Reports arrive. People with acronyms after their names assure everyone that things are under control. The systems know what's going on. The family does not.

Diverging Priorities

To be clear: Institutions are not villains. Human beings need ways to pool knowledge and share labor. And dividing that labor by specializing is what has produced the abundance we now experience, contrasted against 250 years ago, when 90 percent of Americans were farmers.[3] The problem is not that these systems exist; it is that their priorities differ from yours. A school cares about enrollment numbers and liability. A hospital cares about occupancy, regulatory compliance, and the billing codes attached to your chart. A wealth management firm cares about assets under management and client retention. A family office, left to its own devices, cares about keeping the machine humming and its own staff employed. None of these missions is unjustified per se. But none of them aligns neatly with raising your children to become wise, capable adults who can steward freedom across generations.

Once you see that, many well-packaged next-gen offerings look different. Some multifamily offices host retreats for heirs, run financial literacy workshops, and offer mentoring programs or curated trips. On the surface, these are framed as ways to empower the rising generation—and some are sincerely and only that. But they often serve a second, hidden purpose: building relationships with successor clients so that when the founding generation dies, the children will feel comfortable leaving the family capital where it is. The firm's real key performance indicator is not whether your son or daughter becomes more capable but whether they stay.

The same pattern appears among lawyers, accountants, and private banks. Complex structures are drafted "for the benefit of the next generation," but the complexity itself makes the family more dependent on the people who designed them. Children are invited to dinners and seminars so they can "understand the plan." Yet, the subtext is that this plan is far too complicated for anyone but the (current) professionals to manage. Even in education, special tracks for the children of donors or executives come with their own implicit bargain: Trust us with your kids and your money, and we will make sure they stay on the right conveyor belt.

When families outsource autonomy, they are not handing their lives to a neutral force. They are plugging into organizations that, by design, tend to optimize for their own metrics. If the family does not maintain a clear sense of its own aims—and a willingness to say no even when something sounds impressive—the pull toward overreliance is constant. Institutions will gladly wrap more services around your children. They are far less concerned with whether your children ever learn to live without them.

Mo' Money, Mo' Problems?

At this point, it's worth pausing to talk about money's role in agency. Money is not just a store of value. It is stored potential energy (as we'll discuss in the next chapter). It widens the range of actions available to you. With enough capital, you can pay for expertise, hire staff, buy time, and influence outcomes. That is what makes outsourcing so tempting. Why wrestle with a problem when you can pay someone who has already wrestled with a hundred similar ones?

But money does not tell you which actions to take. It does not pick a direction or replace judgment but only amplifies whatever judgment is already present. If the prevailing habit in a family is "let's find someone to handle this," then more wealth means more handling. If the habit is "let's understand this well enough to decide what to do, even if we bring in help," then more wealth means more reach for thoughtful action.

The point is not that everyone in a wealthy family needs to become an expert in tax law or portfolio theory. The point is that someone in the family needs to own the questions. Someone needs to sit across from the advisor and say, "Explain this to me until I can say it back in my own words." Someone needs to say to a school, "This is what we expect from our children's education." Someone needs to ask a doctor, "What are the trade-offs here, and what happens if we choose not to follow this path?" If no one in the family plays that role, the only stories their children will see are stories of passive consumption and quiet compliance.

Huguette Clark's story compresses these tendencies into something almost allegorical. She had roughly half a billion dollars (inflation adjusted) and a staff willing to carry out any request. Over time, the people she interacted with most were not peers or protégés but nurses, housekeepers, and contractors. Her world shrank to a handful of transactional, nonfamilial relationships and a pile of assets that never demanded much of her beyond instruction. She remained intellectually sharp, but she lived in a way that required almost no human courage. Her financial capital allowed her to do that. It also ensured that whatever human capital might have been developed around her was orphaned.

It's pretty unlikely that you are in danger of secluding yourself into complete dependency on a few members of your family's staff. But the pressures that shaped Huguette's life are all around us in softer forms. When you can hire a coach for every weakness, hire an expert for every problem, put your children in programs for every gap, and connect through screens instead of faces, drifting into a pattern where the family's main job is merely to make decisions and authorize payments becomes very easy.

Agency does not survive that pattern for long. Neither does meaning.

If comfort is the solvent we examined in the first chapter, then institutions are the containers that catch whatever melts. The question for any family with means is whether they will simply let that happen or insist on remaining the primary architects of their own human capital. Institutions can help. They can carry pieces of the load. They cannot raise your children into people who know how to think, choose, and build.

That work still belongs to you. Institutions can support a family in building human capital capabilities, but if they *become* the human capital capability, the family no longer has any. No institution, no matter how skilled or well-meaning, can take over the work without depriving the family of its capability—and turning parents from builders into bystanders.

Clarity Through Motion

If your family is going to reclaim that work, you cannot wait until everything feels clear. You have to move first and let clarity catch up. Like Claiborne, you can't think your way out of the problem. You have to begin acting.

Most people imagine agency as something you either have or don't have—a fixed trait. In practice, it behaves more like a cycle. You notice something, you act, you get a response, you learn, and the following action is a little sharper. Your agency expands as you take action and spin up more cycles. Over time, those actions and their feedback build both competence and conviction. The families we see who retain a strong sense of direction in an institutional age are not the ones who spend the most time planning. They are the ones who keep this cycle turning. They just keep doing things.

You can think of the cycle as a simple flywheel (see figure 5). One point on the circle is observation. You see a problem or an opportunity. Next comes action—some small step, not a complete solution. Then, feedback, as reality pushes back or responds. (To use the language in our first chapter, this feedback is some sort of reflection of the value created by that action, positive or negative.) This reflection, as an output of your experiment of action, produces insight. And the insight becomes an input for your next experiment of action. As we cycle through experiments, those insights gradually bring additional clarity to the originating observation, transforming it into a vision for the future and a belief in who we can become. The wheel doesn't stop there. That clarity shapes a newfound perspective, what you become capable of observing next, what new actions you try, and how you interpret the results. This cycle is the engine that powers the compounding of human capital.

THE CLARITY FLYWHEEL

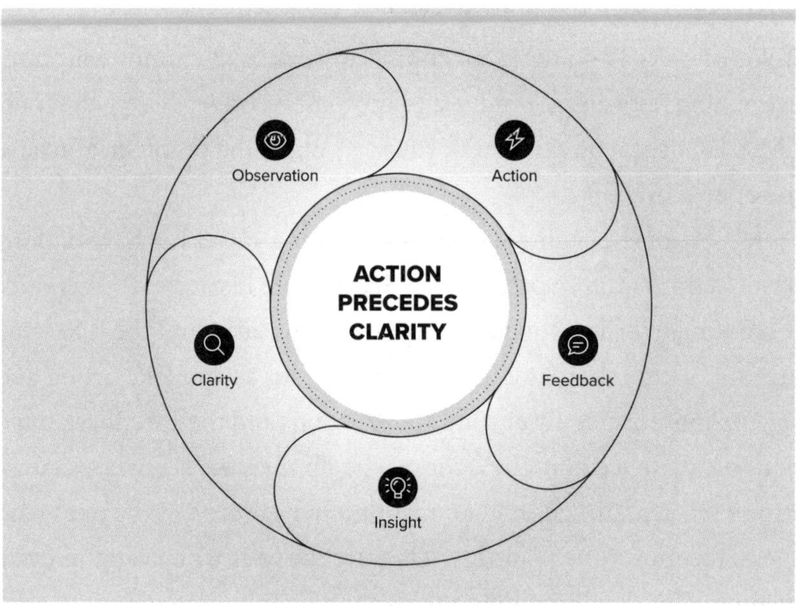

Figure 5

Families often invert this order. They wait for clarity before moving. They postpone decisions about education, philanthropy, or community engagement until they have "the right strategy" or "the full picture." In the meantime, they continue to default to whatever institutions recommend. The flywheel never starts. Agency stays theoretical, and the family remains disempowered.

The only way to get out of that posture is to accept that the first few turns of the wheel will feel clumsy. The first time you sit down with your children to talk about the family's use of money, the conversation will probably feel awkward. The first time you ask an advisor to explain a structure in plain language, you may feel out of your depth. (Thankfully, AI chatbots won't make you feel stupid when asking questions!) The first time you tell a child to call a teacher instead of doing it yourself, the silence at the end of the line may be uncomfortable. But those are the moments where agency begins to reappear. You are choosing to act rather than to let a system act for you.

Chad Willardson has seen this with his client families and his own five kids. He founded Pacific Capital, a wealth advisory firm for ultra-high-net-worth families, and his own success has forced him to think hard about how to build human capital alongside financial capital. When his children were young, he and his wife decided there would be no automatic allowance—no weekly entitlement pay simply for existing. Instead, he put a "menu of opportunity" on the fridge: unpaid tasks that came with being part of the family, alongside a list of optional jobs with dollar amounts next to each. If the kids wanted money, they picked from the list and did the work. If they didn't, they went without.

Chad continued that pattern as his children grew older. When his two oldest asked what they should do with their savings, he didn't take the money, disappear into a bank, and hand them account numbers. He drove them to a branch, walked them to the lobby, and then stepped back. They turned around, nervous, and asked what they were supposed to say. He told them it was their money and their errand. They would have to find the words. They stammered through the conversation with the teller. They answered questions they barely understood. They signed forms. They left lighter in the hands and heavier in experience.

This task would have been quicker and tidier if Chad had handled it for his kids. It would also have reinforced the message that interacting with financial systems is something adults do on their own behalf. Instead, they got a value reflection they still talk about years later: the memory of having been treated as someone who could walk up to a counter, explain what they wanted, and see a transaction completed. They had agency.

Later, when Chad's teenage daughter wanted to join a humanitarian trip to Africa, the same logic applied. It would have been less hassle, and well within his means, to pay the entire cost. Instead, he sat with her and mapped out what it would take for her to fund a significant portion on her own. A basic job with low pay wouldn't get her there in time. That exercise forced her to ask a different kind of question: not "Who will pay for this?" but "What do I know how to do that's valuable enough to get there faster?" That value-creation approach led her to design a backyard basketball clinic, market it to younger players, and earn many times the hourly rate of that first job she'd considered. The trip didn't just happen to her (or for her). She helped make it happen. She, too, had agency.

These are small actions taken in low-risk circumstances. But they can profoundly alter a child's sense of agency and their later interactions with institutions eager to lighten their load.

Chad's kids will still use banks, schools, employers, and programs, but they have early memories of initiating action and designing their own path forward. That makes it much harder for them to see every system as something that does things for them, and much easier to see those systems as tools they can engage and direct. In a world where affluent families are constantly told, "Let us handle it," those early experiences of handling it themselves are the difference between being lifelong clients and becoming adults who expect to stay at the center of their own lives.

Taylor's story with No Name Ventures shows this same pattern in a different setting. At twenty-nine, after becoming a partner at a venture studio, he wanted to start investing in the companies he worked with and believed in. He had already gained experience as a founder, worked with other founders, and built a network in the early-stage venture landscape. The standard move for someone in his position would have been to make the investments himself and ask the family office to allocate additional capital to fund his desire to invest. Many offices would have done precisely that, in part to keep the assets in-house and to empower a member of the next generation to steward family capital. It would have been the far-right side of the graph in action.

Instead, when he sat down with the family office's president to discuss investing his own capital in three start-ups, he received more than just feedback. The president acknowledged the merit of the investments and said the family might also want to participate. But then he added a condition: Taylor would also have to raise outside capital from third parties. If he could do that—if he could convince other investors to partner with him—then the family office would consider investing alongside as well. So rather than personally investing in a few start-ups or investing on behalf of the family office, Taylor started a venture firm and formed a venture fund.

The discussion with the president achieved several critical ends. It refused to put Taylor on a leash or a stipend. It protected the integrity of the existing capital while opening the door for him to build on it. The president's decision treated the family office as an ally in Taylor's agency, not as a replacement for it. Taylor's ambition expanded, and he was provided tangible direction for action. Taylor couldn't just write a check; he had to take action to get nonfamilial feedback, gain insight to clarify, and observe a better approach to make the investments more viable and marketable. The flywheel was engaged.

Taylor left that meeting energized. Nobody had told him no. But nobody had given him a blank check either. He now had a path, and that path ran straight through skills he did not yet possess: raising money from strangers, writing investment memos that could withstand scrutiny, building a thesis coherent enough to attract limited partners, sourcing additional investment opportunities, and building a brand. He could not outsource those challenges but had to grow into them. He had to augment his agency, which would not have happened if his own family's institutional apparatus had simply absorbed his idea and cut a check. He ended up investing in those three companies, and many more, but he had to build a venture firm to do it.

Reclaiming Human Capital

Families must reclaim the right and responsibility to shape their own human capital—the mix of skills, habits, courage, worldview, and relational depth that determines how a person moves through the world and, potentially, shapes it. Unlike financial capital, it cannot be handed down in a document. Human capital is built slowly, through exposure and effort. You cannot hire someone else to provide it on your family's behalf.

Yet that is precisely what many families try to do. They hire schools to handle intellectual development, sports programs to handle toughness, churches or camps to handle morality, therapists to handle emotional resilience, and advisors to handle financial wisdom. There is nothing inherently wrong with any of those roles, but none of them shares your incentive to raise a well-rounded builder, let alone create a chain of positive outcomes for your descendants fifty or a hundred years from now. Only the family has that kind of stake.

That is why the family has to stay at the center of the flywheel. Institutions can be part of the action and feedback. They cannot be allowed to own the capability that develops human capital. If you outsource that capability, you lose it and will get whatever those systems are built to produce: compliant workers, satisfied customers, or recurring revenue. You will not necessarily get entrepreneurial builders who act with purpose and passion. You will get dependents.

Reclaiming this role does not mean sacking the family office staff, pulling children out of school, and firing every professional you work with. It means moving back toward the sweet spot on that agency curve and staying there on purpose. It means asking, in each domain, "Where have we slid further right than we intended?" and "What would one step back to the left look like that still makes sense in our actual lives?"

In education, for example, one step back might be as simple as entering your child's learning world instead of treating school as a sealed box. That can look like sitting with them over homework now and then, asking what they're reading, and building a shared vocabulary at home for the ideas they're encountering. Teachers universally agree that academic outcomes improve and confidence rises when parents stay engaged. As you understand what's being taught, you can decide where to echo it, where to add context, and where to push back. Strengthening your child's agency might mean nudging them to ask clarifying questions, challenge a teacher's assumption, or point out an error respectfully, instead of silently absorbing everything as if it must be true because it came from the authority figure.

In money, one step back might be pulling your adult children into genuine reviews of the family's structures, rather than putting them on "need-to-know" status until a triggering event. That does not mean explaining every technical detail. It does mean giving them a chance to ask questions and to see that you are willing to say, "I don't know; let's find out." It also means gradually shifting some decisions into their hands with appropriate guardrails, so that they are not inheriting both capital and responsibility cold.

In work and contribution, one step back might be requiring that every able-bodied child or grandchild have some form of responsibility outside the home—paid or unpaid—before they finish high school. Not because they need the income, but because you want them to experience themselves as useful in a context where you are not the one who loves them by default. When a coach, boss, or client reflects back to them that their effort mattered, it builds a kind of confidence that nothing inside the family can fully duplicate.

In your relationship with advisors, one step back might be to start asking for explanations instead of simply nodding along. If your wealth manager uses a term you don't understand, you stop the conversation and ask them to define it. If your estate attorney recommends a structure, you ask plain-language questions about what would happen under different scenarios. You do not need to become a professional in their field. You do need to model curiosity and a willingness to engage.

You can also build structures inside the family that support this posture. A weekly family council, like the one Chad holds, can be a simple way for children to discuss decisions they face, for parents to share what they are working on, and for everyone to practice talking about priorities, trade-offs, and plans. Annual vision sessions can give older children a chance to voice what they want the following year to be about and to hear what their parents are aiming for as well. These rhythms do not need to be elaborate. Their power lies in repetition. They keep the family's own aims in view, even as the world around you keeps offering ready-made scripts. (Again, more on these concepts in chapter 8.)

None of this guarantees that your children will choose well. Agency is not the same as control. In fact, reclaiming family agency often means giving up the illusion of control that comes from letting institutions dictate everything. It is easier, in the short term, to do what everyone else in your segment of society is doing and to trust that the machine will produce the outcomes you want. It is harder to step back, notice the machine's direction (and examples of its output), and decide where you want to cooperate and where you want to resist.

But that is what families who preserve freedom do. They decide.

In an institutional age, the family has two options. It can become a client of powerful systems and hope that those systems care enough about its long-term well-being. Alternatively, it can use those systems as specialized tools that can be leveraged by the system that *you* build, own, and control. The first path leads, gradually, toward a version of Huguette Clark's life: heavily managed, well supplied, but thinly rooted in human connection and growth. The second path is messier. It requires more conversation, more practice, more willingness to wrestle with things you could easily pay someone else to handle. It requires building.

It is also the only path that leaves your descendants with more than empty houses and polished reports. Your descendants instead leave with stories, scars, skills, and the sense that they come from a line of people who did not simply go along. They leave with the inner posture that says, "This is our life. We intend to live it with our eyes open."

In a world eager to take over, how much are you prepared to reclaim?

Principles

1. **Outsourced autonomy erodes character.** When families let schools, advisors, and other systems make all the hard calls, children never have to face discomfort, negotiate, or own the consequences of their choices. They may grow up surrounded by competence, but they don't develop much of their own. Over time, they learn to see themselves as passengers in well-run machines, rather than people expected to think and act.

2. **Families must reclaim the right and responsibility to shape their own human capital.** No institution shares your stake in who your children become decades from now; only the family cares about descendants it will never meet. That means parents can't outsource the work of building courage, judgment, and skills to schools, firms, or apps. They have to stay at the center—deciding what to accept, what to resist, and how to give their kids real chances to act, struggle, and grow.

Application Examples

These ideas matter most when translated from concept to concrete action. Below is a sampling of age-appropriate prompts to guide you with your children or grandchildren.

Get the full list at WealthTrapBook.com/list.

- **Ages 5–8**

  Let them help decide on a Saturday activity, a dessert, or which park to visit, and then follow through. Ask, "Make a choice and tell us why you picked it." This gives low-stakes practice in choosing, not just complying.

- **Ages 9–12**

  When a school issue or scheduling problem arises, have them email or speak with the teacher or coach first. You can help draft the message, but their name should be on it. Debrief afterward: "How did it feel? What would you say differently next time?"

- **Ages 13–17**

  Require at least one job or regular commitment: summer work, babysitting, mowing lawns, refereeing kids' games—anything where someone other than you is counting on them. The point is not income, but gaining ownership over something.

- **Ages 18–25**

  Ask them to propose and lead a value-creating initiative. This could be within the family (a new giving strategy), within a company (a process improvement), or in the community (a project or event). They should write a short plan: what, why, cost, and expected impact. Approve it if it's reasonable, and let them run it.

CHAPTER 3

Money as Stored Energy

On Christmas week in 2002, Andrew "Jack" Whittaker Jr. walked into a convenience store in West Virginia, bought a Powerball ticket, and woke up a few days later as the owner of one of the largest lottery jackpots in history. He was already doing well for himself; his construction company employed hundreds of people, and he was worth millions before the ticket. But the winning numbers turned his life into something else entirely. He took the lump sum—roughly $113 million after taxes—and was flown with his family to New York on a private jet to tour a parade of morning shows for interviews and talk about what he planned to do with the money.

Whittaker didn't sound like a cartoon villain gloating about his win, nor was he the stereotypical middle- or low-class person finally striking it rich. He talked about building churches, feeding people, and providing clothing for children. Within months, he had poured millions into church construction and charitable efforts. He started a foundation. He donated large sums to local causes. He spoke as someone who thought he understood money and was prepared for the complications it creates. Then the other shoe dropped.

Requests poured in by the thousands. The mailroom at his foundation spent hours each day just opening envelopes. People stopped him in parking lots and at gas stations. Strangers called his home and showed up at his business. Some asked politely; many did not. Every relative, distant acquaintance, and passerby had a story about why they should be next in line. Lawsuits began to land on his desk. Over four hundred legal claims were filed against him or his company in the years after his win.

Predators showed up as well. One night, someone broke into his vehicle and made off with a briefcase containing a few hundred thousand dollars in cash and several hundred thousand more in cashier's checks. Other thefts followed. There were reports that his accounts had been drained by fraud. At the same time, his own habits began to shift. He drank more. He gambled more. He spent more time with people and in places that did not have his long-term well-being in mind.

The human cost was sharper than the financial. A teenage granddaughter began using drugs and became entangled with people who saw Whittaker's name as an opportunity. A friend of hers was found dead of a drug overdose at his house. Months later, the granddaughter herself was gone, the circumstances of her death murky and painful. Years afterward, when reporters asked him about the win, he said, "I wish I'd torn that ticket up." He continued, "Since I won the lottery, I think there is no control for greed. I think if you have something, there's always someone else that wants it."[1]

It is tempting to turn Whittaker into a morality tale about sudden wealth: easy come, easy go. It's undoubtedly a stereotypical outcome for lottery winners and the like who struggle to manage the massive life changes that follow. But that misses the point. Whittaker was not a naive kid or inexperienced adult—he was a middle-aged builder who had already made money the hard way. He started with sincere intentions. What his story really shows is what can happen when an enormous amount of financial energy hits a system that wasn't designed to handle that level of voltage. Some of what came out was constructive; much of it was chaos.

Money Is Stored Energy

This is how money behaves. It's not a trophy or an idle asset. It is stored energy.

Think of the electric box in your house. The power coming into it is dangerous. Without breakers and wiring, it can burn the place down. With the proper infrastructure—insulation, breakers, and grounded lines—it silently runs lights, refrigerators, computers, and heat. The electricity hasn't changed. The system that handles it has.

Money works the same way. It is energy that needs to be directed, that needs to flow somewhere. Money will power something, amplifying whatever story, habits, and character it flows through. When the system is strong, that energy becomes creation. When the system is weak or undefined, the same energy escapes through every crack—addictions, status games, parasitic relationships, or frantic attempts to fix problems that weren't there before.

That's why thinking of wealth only in terms of size is misleading. People tend to talk about money in terms of totals: net worth, portfolio value, or the size of a trust. They treat it as if judging a vehicle based on the size of its gas tank. More gallons somehow equals more horsepower.

But a race car with a huge tank and a weak engine is still going to be passed up by everyone else. What really matters is what sits under the hood. Human capital is the engine: the ability to identify opportunities, solve problems, build things, recover from setbacks, and create value for others. Financial capital is fuel. If the engine is strong, the fuel will be put to great use, enabling amazing things. If the engine is weak, the size of the gas tank won't matter.

Elon Musk was once asked what he would do if he somehow lost it all and had to start over with a mere thousand dollars—how would he operate his proverbial engine if the tank was effectively empty? His reply demonstrates that the capacity to utilize energy effectively is far more critical than the present amount of stored energy:

> I have a lot of knowledge . . . It's impossible for someone to have that amount of all the knowledge that I have and then be dropped down to a low resource amount . . . I will be able to ask people to just give me money. And with the promise that I will have a high return, which is what I'm able to do right now. If you give me a dollar, you will get back much more than a dollar.[2]

Elon's point was that his real wealth is his capacity to build. Capital is magnetically drawn to that. The tank follows the engine.

This matters for families because it flips the standard script. Most planning assumes that the job is to preserve as much fuel as possible for future generations. We obsess over the tank: how big it is, how to shield it from taxes, how to make sure nobody pokes holes in it. Meanwhile, very little attention is paid to the engine's condition. If your children inherit a massive reservoir of stored energy without having developed the ability to harness and direct it, you haven't blessed them. You've put them behind the wheel of something they're not trained to drive.

The question, then, isn't simply, "How much money will we pass on?" It's, "What are we doing to build the kind of people who can use that energy without it burning them?"

One way to think about that question is through the lens of value reflections. We previously explored how our children come to understand themselves, as we all do, by seeing how the world responds to their actions. When they do something, their environment reflects something back. Praise, resistance, indifference, gratitude, resentment—each response teaches them what kinds of effort matter and what kinds don't.

Money is often woven into those reflections. When you deploy capital, the world responds. Sometimes it responds with more capital. Sometimes it responds with appreciation, impact, or changed lives. Sometimes it responds with silence and other times with pain.

The Value Reflection Matrix (see figure 6) is a simple way to make sense of these interactions. On one axis are positive versus negative reflections: Did your environment respond with a reward or a setback? On the other axis is whether the outcome was meaningful or meaningless. Cross those two dimensions, and four quadrants emerge.

Positive reflections in an area that isn't meaningful produce hollow achievement. For a child, that might be the A-plus grade earned in a class they couldn't care less about, or the participation trophy that sits on the shelf but isn't tied to anything meaningful inside them. It looks impressive from the outside and photographs well, but it doesn't change who they believe themselves to be or who they are capable of becoming. Negative reflections in an area that isn't meaningful are simply noise—like failing to smile for the family photo they don't want to take, or being yelled at for not practicing an instrument they never wanted to play and don't feel any connection to. The experience doesn't build character; it just teaches withdrawal.

The other side of the matrix is where identity actually gets built. When a child receives a positive value reflection in an area that genuinely matters to them, it becomes a peak moment—a life-enhancing experience we'll explore more in chapter 9. Think of a kid who cares deeply about animals and uses their own saved money and some of yours to launch a small dog-walking business in the neighborhood. The first time a neighbor thanks them, pays them, and asks them to come back, that turns ordinary income into evidence that who they are and what they did had real value. Or a teenager who organizes a battle of the bands and sees younger kids participate and enjoy it; that memory will shape how they see themselves for years to come. Peak moments transform our perspective on what we believe we are capable of and who we believe we can become.

Negative reflections in meaningful areas are different. They hurt, but they are rich in information. These are key learnings. You might invest alongside your teenager in a business they're excited about, only to watch it fail. You might fund a project that fits your family's mission, only to see it sputter or get mismanaged. Perhaps your child organizes a service project where only two volunteers show up. If you're willing to sit in the discomfort and debrief honestly—what did we miss, what did we assume, what did we learn about ourselves, and so on—then those losses stop feeling like verdicts on who they are and start functioning as tuition for who they're becoming.

When you examine how your family has used money in the past decade, you can probably drop each significant outlay into one of these quadrants. Some experiences were wins you barely remember because they didn't matter. Some pursuits were flops that might have bothered you, but didn't warrant changed behavior. Some created stories you tell with pride. And there might be a few stories, the peak moments, that changed everything. The point of the matrix is to get a clearer view of whether your stored energy is creating the most value it can. The matrix also raises a practical question: Given the energy in your system, where is it flowing now, and are we striving to maximize the frequency and amplitude of peak moments?

VALUE REFLECTION MATRIX

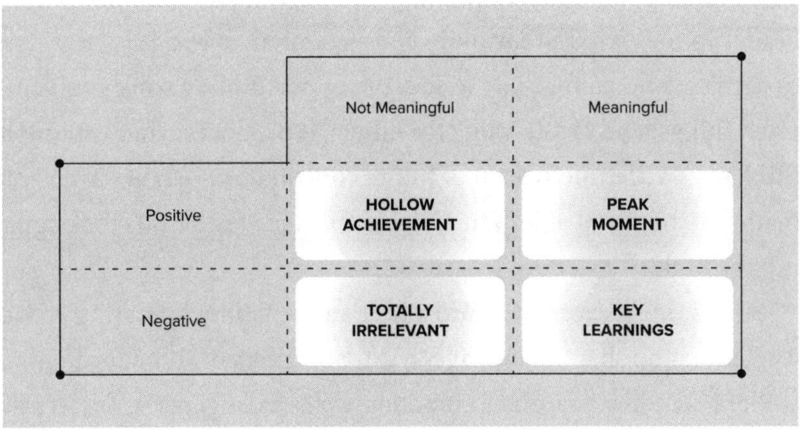

Figure 6

The Uses of Capital

Most families, when they look honestly at their finances, see money moving through a few familiar channels. They spend, they save, and they give. But that surface view misses the real question. Instead of asking, "Where did the money go?" ask, "What did the money *become*?"

If capital is stored energy, then when it leaves your account, it doesn't merely purchase things—it shapes behavior. Behavior compounds into capability. Capability hardens into identity. And identity, multiplied across people, becomes culture. That is why the uses of capital are not just categories of spending. They are what you might call *value derivatives*, where each use creates a different order of value, and the orders are not equal.

Some uses of money create what we could call zero-order value: immediate comfort. The nice dinner, the upgraded seat, the new gadget. These aren't bad, but their value is consumed in the moment and doesn't compound. Some uses create first-order value: financial return. You deploy capital, and more capital comes back. This is what most people mean when they talk about "investing." It grows the tank.

Some uses create second-order value: human capability. This is harder to measure but far more consequential. When capital is used to develop a person's ability to identify opportunities, solve problems, build things, and create value for others, it produces what you might think of as a lifetime stream of future contribution—their capacity to matter in the world, compounding across decades. This is the engine, not the tank.

And some uses create third-order value: family operating capacity. This is the shared language, trust, governance, and coordination ability that allow a family to function well across generations. It's the cultural infrastructure that determines whether your grandchildren will be able to work together on hard problems or whether they'll hire lawyers to fight over the scraps. Within these value derivatives, or uses of capital, we can classify most financial behavior into five channels.

The first is consumption: money used for lifestyle—homes, travel, restaurants, hobbies, entertainment, toys. Consumption is not automatically shallow. Some of the best uses of capital live here, such as trips that bond your family, meals that create a breakthrough conversation, or environments that expose your children to ideas and people they would never otherwise encounter. That is meaningful consumption. It doesn't just create pleasure; it also creates memory. And memory, transferred through story, is a multigenerational asset. A meaningful trip can become a family story that lasts decades as an identity anchor ("This is the kind of family we are"). But there is another form: consumption with no story attached, such as purchasing to signal status, upgrades that don't change anyone's life, spending meant to numb, distract, or defer discomfort. This kind of spending creates a dangerous derivative: It trains a person to equate money with escape. You don't need to feel guilty about every purchase, obviously. But you do need to notice patterns. If most of your outflow is oriented toward comfort with no higher aim—no learning, no contribution, no relationship—then your children will not infer that money is a tool for meaning. They will infer that money is a tool for self-indulgence.

The second channel is strategic reserves: capital held as optionality. Every wise system needs reserves—runway to endure shocks, to act quickly when an opportunity appears, to support a transition, to fund a season of apprenticeship or entrepreneurship. This is not hoarding because reserves have a stated purpose. They exist to preserve freedom of action and to act as a reserve for flow. Hoarding is energy stored *instead of* flow.

So let's now address hoarding, the third channel: accumulating assets without any clear purpose beyond accumulation itself. It can look prudent on the surface— "compounding," "staying conservative," or "keeping options open"—but often it is anxiety dressed up as discipline. Underneath the justification may sit a quiet belief that no matter how much there is, it might not be enough. Or a fear that your descendants cannot be trusted to use it well. That fear keeps capital sitting in the gas tank, not because there is no current use for it, but because imagining those uses forces you to confront uncertainty—about the future, about your heirs, and about whether your judgments will hold up in the open. In our energy metaphor, hoarding is like buying pallets of batteries and leaving them shrink-wrapped in the garage forever. The label still says "fully charged." But over time, the chemistry degrades. Stored energy that never flows slowly loses its capacity—and becomes, in a sense, meaningless. The tragedy of hoarding is not that it fails to maximize returns. The tragedy is that it fails to maximize *capability*. It prevents capital from doing what it uniquely can do: creating higher-order value in people and systems.

The fourth channel is transactional allocation: writing checks to causes, investments, or organizations because they are respectable, because your circle does it, or because your parents always gave and you feel obligated to keep the tradition alive. It might be gifts to a university, contributions at a gala, or LP commitments to a fund—mainly so your name is on the list and you're seen in the right rooms. There is nothing inherently wrong with any of it. But if these flows occur without relationship, study, participation, or follow-through, they often produce a thin derivative: reputation without transformation. Your children see money leaving and praise returning, but they don't see you wrestling with the problem, learning the domain, walking with the people involved, or building something useful. There is little tuition in this. It produces external affirmation without internal formation.

Finally, there is capability investment: capital deployed to build people. This is money used to fund experiments, apprenticeships, training, ventures, service, and seasons of focused work. It is not bailout capital. It is not comfort capital. It is *formation* capital. It can look like funding a child's first serious experiment, enrolling them in a training program, covering living expenses while they build a business, or covering the costs of a multimonth service activity in a developing nation. A capability investment can include a prototype budget, travel to learn a craft, or the tools required to produce something real. Sometimes that's as concrete as a 3-D printer and a weekend market (see KidsMarkets.com). Sometimes it's an unconventional path toward professional success instead of pursuing a credential (see JoinPraxis.com). You cannot model this cleanly in a spreadsheet to show the internal rate of return of funding a young person to attempt a first venture or launch a small project. You may never be able to prove that the money "beat the market." But that objection assumes the wrong definition of wealth. If the true definition of wealth is the ability to create value for others, then the most essential use of stored energy is to increase that ability in the people you are responsible for.

This is where the second-order derivative dominates: capability compounding. When capability investment goes well, it produces peak moments that shape identity—for the person funded, the supporters, the next generation watching, and future generations who will inherit the story. And when it does not go as hoped, the "losses" often sit in the key-learning quadrant—provided you tell the truth about what happened. The energy did not vanish but moved into the person's wisdom reservoir. The energy becomes judgment, pattern-recognition, humility, grit, and discernment—assets that are invisible on a balance sheet but decisive over a lifetime.

There is risk here, of course. People have agency. They can squander opportunities and walk away from paths you thought were promising. That is why many families retreat to safer-feeling uses of capital: more hoarding, more transactional allocation, more gifts to institutions whose prestige feels like proof that the money was "used responsibly." But the uncomfortable truth remains: no foundation, fund, or building has ever created value on its own. People always did the thinking and acting. Energy flows best into *people* who are building the capacity to use it well. And when those people do not exist—or when we refuse to build them—stored energy becomes not merely idle, but corrosive. The family grows richer in the first-order sense and poorer in the second and third.

A family that wants to last must care about all three ledgers: the lifestyle ledger, which tracks comfort and celebration; the financial ledger, which tracks returns and resilience; and the capability ledger, which tracks human capital and the family system that protects and multiplies it. Because in the end, money is not the point. Money is the *medium*. What matters is what it becomes—inside people, across time.

Mapping Your Time

If individuals are the source of value, then the way you and your children spend your time and attention is just as important as where you park your capital. Money is stored energy; time and attention are live current. They reveal how you're actually directing energy day to day—and how much of it might be wasting away like batteries on a shelf, no matter what your intentions once were.

Most families have never intentionally mapped this out. They feel busy, but they don't know where the hours are going. They say that family, health, or service matter, but they can't show you what those words look like on a weekly calendar. If you want to steer financial energy toward capability instead of comfort—if you want your kids to be active builders instead of passive beneficiaries—you need a clear view of how the family's energy is flowing and a shared language on how to discuss it.

One way to get that view is through a simple exercise we call the Energy Allocation Lens (see figure 7). The idea is straightforward: Every week, you have a finite allocation of waking hours. Assume roughly sixteen hours a day, seven days a week—that's 112 hours. This is your stack of batteries for the week. You can spend them however you like, but you don't get more. If they idle, they waste away.

Take a piece of paper or a simple spreadsheet and create a row for each domain of meaning that matters in each person's life (we recommend doing this as a family activity with each person filling it out for themselves): family and relationships, work/building, health, growth/learning, faith/service/community. Add a line at the bottom called "unallocated/drift" to capture whatever isn't going anywhere in particular. Then make two columns: ideal hours and actual hours.

Start with the *ideal* column. If you could spend those same 112 waking hours in a way that reflected who you want to become and what you want your family to stand for, what would the numbers look like? You may wish to spend two more hours a week with your spouse, three more in the gym, and fewer evenings frittered away with entertainment or work emails. Maybe you realize that all your "service" is writing checks and that you'd like to spend at least a few hours a month doing something hands-on with your children for the experience and relationships. Be intentional but realistic about what your true ideal looks like. And it's okay to have unallocated hours; we humans are not purely productive robots every hour of every day—and having unstructured time, particularly for younger children, is essential.

Then fill in the *actual* column. Use your calendars to calculate how much time each of you really spent last week in each domain. (If last week was anomalous compared to your average schedule, then pick another week.) How many hours went into focused work? How many into your marriage, your kids, your friends? How much exercise did you actually get? How many hours disappeared into scrolling, mindless TV, or aimless puttering? Add up the totals for each domain, then subtract them from 112. Whatever is left is *drift*.

When you're done, subtract actual from ideal in each row. A positive number means that perhaps too little energy flowed into that meaning domain, presenting an opportunity for greater allocation in the future. A negative number indicates an overallocation and may need to be dialed back. The math isn't complicated, but it forces you to confront trade-offs we often avoid. Every extra hour spent in one area has to come from somewhere else.

ENERGY ALLOCATION LENS

Simple Entry + Delta — Weekly budget: **112 hours (16x7)**

Domain	Ideal (hrs/wk)	Actual (hrs/wk)	Delta=Ideal–Actual
Family & Relationships	–	–	–
Work / Creation	–	–	–
Health	–	–	–
Growth / Learning	–	–	–
Faith / Service / Community	–	–	–
Unallocated / Drift (112 - total)	–	–	–
TOTAL	**112**	**112**	**0**

Figure 7

As you compare your results against your spouse's or children's, you'll see, in black and white, how each person currently distributes their energy, and how they wish they were distributing it. You may find that your teenager wants more time learning and less time in organized activities, or that your spouse feels starved for time with you, while you imagined the opposite. You may discover that as a family, you're spending a stunning number of hours and dollars on leisure or work, while drift quietly eats the margin where deeper conversations might have taken place.

Once those numbers are on the table, money starts to look different. It is no longer just something to preserve. It becomes a lever you can use to shift your energy out of drift and toward your ideal. If you realize you're spending ten hours a week on logistics you could pay someone else to handle, and you also know you're starving other domains that matter more, suddenly the cost of a part-time assistant or a different schooling arrangement isn't just an expense. It's a way to reallocate current. On the other hand, if you see that you are already spending heavily on things that don't move any of your domains toward ideal, you may decide to let those flows taper.

This is where the earlier four channels of capital—consumption, hoarding, transactional allocation, and investment in individuals—stop being abstract buckets and start showing up on your calendar. They're no longer just ideas on a whiteboard; they're how you and your kids actually spend hours and dollars each week. It helps to remember that you and your family members are not the battery. The money is. Your roles are closer to that of a grid operator: You decide where the current runs, how strong it is in each line, and which transformers it passes through on the way. You're responsible for building an energy grid that can move capital from where it's generated to the people, projects, and experiences where it can be safely converted into real work, growth, and value.

Take the archetype of the hoarder. A friend of Taylor's lives well but far below his means. He spends perhaps two million a year, earns ten times that, and piles the difference into accounts he rarely touches. On a balance sheet, this may look impressive: The tank keeps getting larger. But if you ran his life through the Energy Allocation Lens, you (and he) might see something else. Work and building would consume the bulk of his hours. Health and relationships might get a modest slice. Growth, learning, and service could show up as almost rounding errors. Drift would be low—not because he's deliberate, but because nearly everything is aimed at maintaining or increasing the pile.

What's more, this man informed his children that they would receive no inheritance. He gives little thought to where the capital will go when he dies; perhaps a foundation or a hotel wing will one day bear his name. The point for him is the game itself—the score. That is his right, and his agency empowers him to pursue this path. But from the standpoint of human capital, the batteries he's storing up are sitting on a shelf, wasting away.

No archetype is pure, and most of us carry a bit of each in different seasons. The point is to notice which direction you lean in by default, and what story your children are absorbing as they watch. Are they seeing money used as a scoreboard, as padding, as an anesthetic, as social signaling? Or are they seeing it used as a tool for agency—something that changes what their family can learn, build, and contribute?

When you start to see capital through this lens, education looks different too. Many affluent parents think that paying exorbitant amounts for their children's private schooling is an investment in their children and their future. Sometimes that's true. More often, particularly in the context of credential-heavy paths, it is closer to transactional allocation. You are buying access to a network, a brand, and a piece of paper. Those things can matter. But they don't automatically translate into capability.

Noticing that gap has led to several alternative programs focused on capability over credentials. Peter Thiel's fellowship program, for example, pays young people to drop out of college and work on companies or projects they care about, betting on individuals rather than institutions. Praxis, briefly referenced earlier, helps young adults skip or leave college and directly enter the job market after a six-month bootcamp, learning by doing and building a portfolio of real work. You don't need to send your children to these specific programs to apply the principle. The question is simply: When you fund something in their life, are you paying mainly for them to be stamped and approved by an institution, or for them to be stretched, challenged, and given space to create? One of those uses may be safer in the short term. The other tends to produce better long-term outcomes. One is more focused on expanding the tank; the other prioritizes the engine.

Meaningful Consumption

Money is not the root of evil, and neither is the comfort it can create—but both can feel radioactive when they're used carelessly. If you've built wealth, you will almost certainly consume more than previous generations did. You may live in nicer houses, travel more, and enjoy food, beauty, and rest that your grandparents would have found unimaginable. That can be good (emphasis on the *can*). The question is whether those flows of energy are tied to anything beyond themselves—whether there is greater meaning attached to the consumption. Comfort in the service of a larger purpose can restore and enrich a family; comfort with no purpose attached drifts quickly toward sedation and, often, self-destructive behavior.

When you spend on a family trip because you want your children to see a part of the world they've only read about, and you use that shared experience as a reference point for later conversations, that is meaningful consumption. The same is true if you hire a landscaper, a private chef, or a house cleaner to buy back time that you can reallocate to more intentional parenting and family projects. By contrast, buying the bigger house mainly so you can host the right people and post the right pictures, or leasing a new car every year mostly so no one ever sees you in last year's model, is obviously something else. Your children may not have the vocabulary to name the difference, but they feel it; they can sense when money is funding real connection and growth, and when it's just costuming.

The same pattern shows up in philanthropy and investing. Writing large checks to institutions can make a difference. Hospitals need equipment. Universities need labs. Nonprofits need operating budgets. But if all of your giving happens at arm's length—no real relationship, no engagement with the work, no feedback loop—your kids will not see those dollars as part of a life they're meant to live. They'll experience it as a ritual that signals status, or as a box you check to look good in certain circles. In that case, the giving doesn't soften their hearts; it hardens them toward wealth itself, because they learn to associate money with performance, ego, and posing, not with building or serving.

There is a different way. You can still give to institutions, but you can also set aside a portion of your capital explicitly for investing in people. That might be a "family experiment fund" where children can pitch projects they want to try, with the understanding that they will present afterward on what happened and what they learned. It might be supporting a nephew's apprenticeship, backing a friend's early-stage company not just with money but with mentoring, or paying a talented team member's tuition for a program you believe will change their trajectory.

Those decisions will not always produce clean financial returns. But they will create stories. They will generate meaning. They will produce peak moments and value reflections. They will give the next generation examples of what it looks like when money's energy is used as a tool to expand what people can become. They will become builders, not batteries on a shelf.

Let's return to Jack Whittaker's story. The jackpots he threw at churches and charities in the first months after his win were generous. They were also primarily transactional. He poured stored energy into institutions he had little history with, under the flashing lights of media coverage, with no real plan for how that energy would be absorbed or utilized. At the same time, he had not built the relational or personal infrastructure to handle the other currents that came with the windfall: opportunists, family members under strain, his own appetites. The voltage found weak joints and arced there. His life exploded.

Most readers of this book aren't dreaming about sudden windfalls of their own; they're already wrestling with how to transfer eight- or nine-figure totals over time to children and grandchildren without blowing up what they've built. The questions are the same as in the lottery story, just playing out more quietly: Is the system in and around your family—your routines, expectations, skills, and culture—actually built to handle the current you're feeding into it? If not, the response isn't to fear money or freeze the flow; it's to upgrade the system so that the energy you've created can move through people and structures that are strong enough to use it well.

That is what builders do. They don't obsess over the size of the tank—they focus on the engine. They know that capital comes and goes, deals work and fail, valuations rise and fall. Energy flows and will continue to do so. What endures is who people become and what they can do when given the chance.

When you consider trust structures, next-gen programs, giving strategies, or career paths for your children, keep a single filter in mind: Does this choice expand or shrink their ability to create value for others? If it expands that capacity, even a little, your stored energy is likely flowing in a healthy direction. If it leaves that capacity unchanged—or quietly weakens it—you are polishing the gas tank while the engine sits idle. In the end, money is only power in standby; it is the family's shared sense of meaning and culture—who we are, what we're for, and whom we serve—that tells that power where to go and keeps it from dissolving into drift. Meaning is what matters, and it should be the mandate that governs how your money is used.

Principles

1. **Money is energy waiting to be directed; it takes on the moral and creative character of its stewards.** Money itself is neutral, like electricity or fuel; it simply magnifies whatever it's plugged into. In the hands of builders, it powers projects, people, and service. In the hands of the fearful, aimless, or status-obsessed, the same money feeds drift, dependency, and damage.
2. **Families must reclaim the right and responsibility to shape their own human capital.** No institution shares your stake in who your children become decades from now; only the family cares about descendants it will never meet. That means parents can't outsource the work of building courage, judgment, and skills to schools, firms, or apps. They have to stay at the center—deciding what to accept, what to resist, and how to give their kids real chances to act, struggle, and grow.

Application Examples

These ideas matter most when translated from concept to concrete action. Below is a sampling of age-appropriate prompts to guide you with your children or grandchildren.

Get the full list at WealthTrapBook.com/list.

- **Ages 5–8**

  Create three money jars labeled "enjoy," "build," and "help." Enjoy is for small treats. Build is for something that takes time (a LEGO set, art supplies, etc.). Help is for choosing someone else to benefit. Let them decide where each dollar they earn goes and talk about what each choice makes possible.

- **Ages 9–12**

  Offer to match (1:1, 3:1, or whatever works for your family's situation) any money they put toward building a skill they're interested in—a coding course, drawing class, woodworking, robotics. Explain that you want to invest in helping them grow their abilities, not just enabling the accumulation of stuff.

- **Ages 13–17**

  Create a small annual budget specifically for them to spend on building capabilities: bootcamps, workshops, advanced tools (camera, software, instruments), travel to conferences, and so on. Any request must answer: "What will this help you become better at?"

- **Ages 18–25**

  If you help with a car, housing, or business seed capital, treat it as energy, not entitlement. Ask them: "What are you committing to build over the next few years, and how does this help?" Get a clear answer. Revisit it annually, not to police them, but to keep money and meaning in the same conversation.

CHAPTER 4

The Meaning Mandate

Barbed wire, guard towers, and smokestacks framed a dreary world in Dachau, one of the first concentration camps built by the Nazis. Inside, nearly everything that makes life human had been stripped away. People were unloaded at gunpoint, shaved, numbered, and packed into barracks built for a fraction of their bodies. Winter meant thin uniforms and wooden clogs on frozen mud. Summer meant disease and stench. Hunger was constant; a crust of bread could turn friends into rivals. Work details marched out each day, not knowing who would return. Beatings, arbitrary executions, and selections for the gas chambers were part of the daily routine. In that environment, talk of hope sounded almost obscene. Survival seemed random, and death was everywhere—bodies collapsed throughout the camp or stacked like cordwood near the crematorium.

Interestingly, the men who survived longest were not always the strongest, healthiest, or youngest. Viktor Frankl—the psychiatrist we referenced earlier, whose observations about meaning have shaped our understanding of human resilience—noticed that early. While his body endured the same starvation and cold as everyone else, his mind kept watching. In that dystopian world, every normal incentive had collapsed. Work no longer led to security or fulfillment. Obedience did not guarantee safety. Kindness could be repaid with brutality. Looking at the external conditions alone, there was almost nothing worth enduring for. Yet some people continued to endure.

Frankl observed that the prisoners who held on were usually anchored to something beyond the wire—someone they loved or a work they believed they still had to finish. A wife's face. Children they had not seen for years. In Frankl's case, it was a book manuscript that existed only in memory. These reasons obviously did not change the soup ration or the weather, but they changed the prisoners' internal dialogues. Instead of wondering whether to continue, those with purpose wondered how they could face that person or that work if they quit now. Meaning did not remove suffering. It changed what suffering meant. "In some way," he later wrote, "suffering ceases to be suffering at the moment it finds a meaning."[1] Recall what Nietzsche said: "He who has a *why* to live for can bear almost any *how*."[2]

Most of us will thankfully never face anything close to that level of horror. But the underlying pattern—the way a clear "why" organizes a life—is the same at any scale. Frankl's point was not that only martyrs or saints need meaning. His point was that when everything else is stripped away, meaning is the last line of defense against despair. When a person believes their life has a purpose, hardship becomes something to navigate. When that reason is absent, even comfortable circumstances feel heavier than they should. Meaning functions less like a garnish on top of a good life and more like an internal spine. Without it, everything else sags.

For affluent families, the danger is this: Nothing feels obviously wrong, but sometimes very little feels right. The pantry is full, the schools are good, the vacations are pleasant, and the accounts are healthy. The children grow up with every door technically open to them, but with very little sense of why they might choose one door over another. While enjoying all the abundance, a question forms in them long before they can even articulate it: "What is any of this . . . for?"

This is the meaning crisis of abundance. Instead of coming with headlines or emergencies, it arrives with scrolling, boredom, a low-level ache that surfaces in teenagers as flirtation with hedonistic comforts and in twenty-somethings as a string of half-hearted starts. They can do almost anything; they are not sure why they should do anything in particular. Previously, we've explored how prosperity dissolves necessity, how institutions rush in to manage what families don't, and how money behaves like stored energy. Fortunately, one thing can organize all of that: a sense of meaning strong enough to direct how you manage and use your resources.

Drifting in a Life of Options

You can hear the absence of meaning in the way heirs often talk about their future. Many will say they do not "have" to work, but feel that they "should" do something. They treat work as a courtesy to society or a box to check, not as an expression of who they are. Some respond by opting out entirely and living on autopilot. Others chase various opportunities because they can't think of anything better to pursue. In either case, the feeling is roughly the same: The script is vague, and none of the paths feel like their own.

The remedy is not to throw away all comfort or engineer artificial misery. The way out of the wealth trap is to cultivate something inside a person that is strong enough to draw them into voluntary struggle (a concept we'll explore in depth in chapter 9). Meaning, in that sense, is a self-chosen necessity, the thing that makes you walk away from the path of least resistance because you cannot *not* pursue it.

Taylor's great-grandfather, the Oscar Award–winning filmmaker King Vidor, offers a compelling example. He was born in Galveston, Texas, in 1894 as the heir to a timber empire. The family operated the Miller Vidor Lumber Company, which encompassed land holdings, lumber mills, merchant operations, and associated railroads in the region. The household reflected the entrepreneurial spirit of late-nineteenth-century Texas commerce, centered on resource extraction and trade. His expected path of least resistance was simple: stay, work, and eventually take over the family business. Then motion pictures arrived. King saw his first film at age fifteen and became obsessed with telling stories through film.

In his mid-teens, King worked as a ticket taker and part-time projectionist at one of Galveston's earliest nickelodeons, gaining firsthand exposure to motion pictures. This practical immersion, rather than formal training, expanded his interest in filmmaking, leading him to experiment independently with rudimentary equipment. Exposure to his father's lumber operations acquainted King with mechanical processes, and using the company's various tools sparked an early, self-directed curiosity about technical experimentation. By 1913, King had constructed a basic motion-picture camera, using makeshift materials to capture local events as amateur newsreels. In 1914, at the age of twenty, King cofounded the Hotex Motion Picture Company to produce short films independently of established studios, but he encountered immediate financing and distribution hurdles, prompting him to seek opportunities elsewhere.

Hollywood was not yet a well-defined industry. There were no clear career ladders, no prestigious film schools, and no guarantee of success. The safer plan was obvious: remain where he was, perhaps dabble with cameras as a hobby, and continue in the family business.

He instead cashed out his savings, made a down payment on a Model T, packed what he could fit, and set off from Galveston, Texas, to Los Angeles across 1,600 miles of unpaved roads. No interstate highways or roadside assistance existed at the time. Gas stations were sparse. A mechanical failure in the wrong stretch of empty land could easily become a survival problem. Fortunately, he arrived in California, sold the car to fund his first months, and took whatever work he could get in the studios—carrying cables, moving equipment, watching, networking, and learning.

From the outside, this was not a glamorous move or even obviously rational. He traded a stable life for long odds in an emerging field. But he had reached the point where staying felt more dangerous than leaving. The person who stayed in Texas would, in a real sense, not be him. That sense of internal necessity—*I have to pursue this, or I'll be betraying something important in myself*—is the feeling that pursuing meaning evokes in a person. Achieving the goal becomes crucial to your sense of self, a matter of life or death to the version of yourself you could become if meaning were your aim.

Over time, Vidor became one of the notable directors of his era. He made films that explored war, class, and personal struggle. He experimented with technique, helped shape a new medium, and eventually received an honorary Oscar, presented by Audrey Hepburn to recognize his "incomparable achievements as a cinematic creator and innovator."[3] The meaning of his life was not that golden statue. It was the decades of work between the Model T and the stage, the years of taking on projects because the stories felt important enough to justify the risk.

Stories like King's can feel distant from the world your children are inheriting. They are growing up in a time when comfort is easy to maintain, and moving across the country involves checking airline prices, not selling your vehicle at the city limits. And yet the inner decision is the same. At some point, if their lives are going to matter in any serious way—if they are ever going to become builders rather than beneficiaries—they will have to feel something similar: a pull strong enough to compete with the gravity of ease, and compelling enough to commit to voluntary struggle.

The Anatomy of Meaning

We need a working definition of meaning that helps you, as a parent, recognize and nurture that pull. Meaning is one of those words that gets thrown around so often that it starts to dissolve. It can sound like a vague, inspirational cloud: Follow your passion, find your path, live your truth. That kind of language does your children no favors; it doesn't direct action or inspire thinking. It suggests that meaning is something you stumble upon in a moment of insight and then enjoy without much effort—the garnish on top of the main course.

A more accurate description is far less romantic. Meaning shows up when three things are true at the same time. First, you are building something you care about. Second, your environment is giving you a positive reflection about what you are building. Third, you have a connection to the individuals who benefit from your work. When those three conditions overlap, a person is more likely to perceive their actions as worthwhile. Struggle becomes joyful. (We'll create a shared language around meaning more precisely in chapter 7.)

We must start with building something—creating value for others. The "something" does not have to be a company or a work of high art. It might be a classroom, a family, a small nonprofit, a product line, a research lab, a community initiative, a local business, or a string of recurring events that you take responsibility for. For a child, it might be a microbusiness, a book they write and publish, a podcast, or a dance camp they organize. The point is that there is some output in the world that did not exist until they acted.

Next is the reflection. Building in a vacuum does not generate much meaning. Reality has to talk back. Customers buy, or they don't. People show up or they don't. Teammates stick around or drift away. Mentors critique. Markets punish and reward. My first book, published in 2011, received substantial positive feedback from friends, family, and strangers alike. My second book, by contrast, mostly landed with a thud. The silence that followed was its own kind of feedback, a reminder that not everything I cared about would resonate with others. Then, in 2014, I started writing the *Tuttle Twins* books. Those stories began to generate a volume and intensity of response I had never experienced before—parents writing to say their kids were talking differently at the dinner table, children clutching dog-eared copies at events hoping for an autograph, families telling me how the ideas had changed their conversations. Writing is often lonely, and I had spent plenty of nights staring at a blank screen, wondering if the effort would be worth it. The flood of sincere reactions made the connection between effort and outcome impossible to ignore. Although I enjoyed writing, it now became work that clearly mattered to others, and that realization anchored writing into the core of how I understand my own purpose. I found meaning by building something where that value was positively reflected back to me. The same opportunity exists for all builders—especially your children.

Finally, there is contribution. There must be someone on the other side of the work. A builder who has no sense of who they serve is like an actor playing to an empty house. They may enjoy the movement, but it eventually rings hollow. For kids, that might be running a weekly game night for younger siblings and their friends, tutoring a classmate who keeps failing math, organizing a pickup sports league at the park so kids who didn't make the school team still get to play, or producing a podcast that helps other teens navigate life well. It could be leading music at a youth group, building a Minecraft server for friends, coaching a little-league team, or creating art to share with neighbors. In each case, there are real people who benefit in visible ways, and your child can point to them and say, "I did that for them"—which is very different from doing things only to impress adults, pad a résumé, or because they were required to do so.

You can imagine these three elements as overlapping circles (see figure 8): value creation (what your child builds), a reflection of that value (what works), and contribution (who they served). Where all three intersect, something else appears. Your child begins to experience themselves as an agent rather than a passenger. Effort feels connected to outcomes. Sacrifice feels tied to people. Building is a blessing, and "work" is fun. Identity starts to coalesce around a story far more substantial than the stuff your family owns or what your wealth makes possible.

Most of the low-level misery that appears among affluent young people can be traced to one of these circles being missing. If they are not building anything, then even the best schools and internships will feel like moving through someone else's maze. If they build but never face real feedback—because parents, staff, or institutions cushion every blow—then their sense of self rests on fantasy. If they build and receive feedback but cannot identify for whom they are doing it, their work becomes about performance, not service, and meaning ebbs away.

This understanding clarifies two common confusions. The first confusion is equating meaning with constant positive emotion. Many of the most meaningful tasks you will ever do will feel, in the moment, like tedious work, awkward risk, or outright suffering. Waking up at three in the morning with a newborn is not pleasant. Exercising daily is unpleasant and time-consuming. Grinding through drafts of a book or a product is not glamorous. These moments are meaningful because they are attached to something you have decided is worth the cost. Remember that the path to hell often feels like heaven (short-term gratification, indulgence, dopamine hits, and hedonism) while the path to heaven often feels like hell (long-term gratification, sacrifice, struggle, discipline, and meaning).

THE ANATOMY OF MEANING

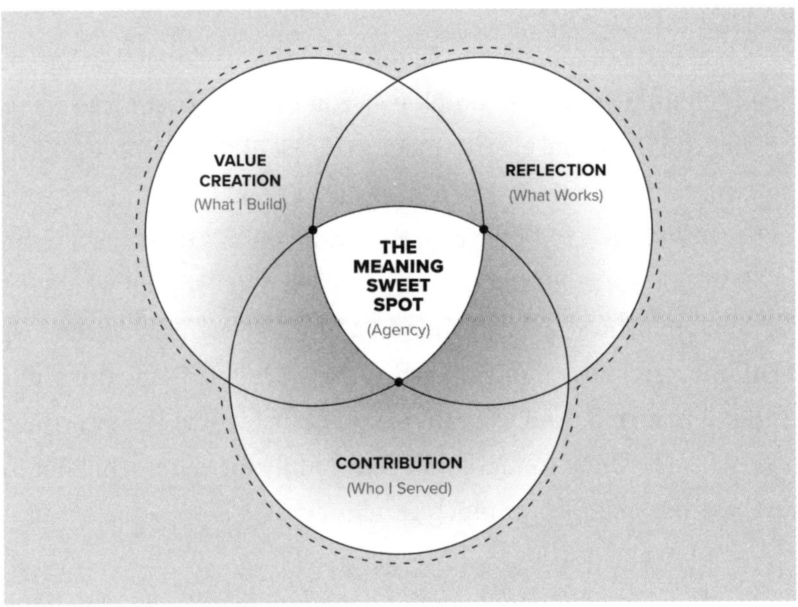

Figure 8

The second confusion arises from attempting to start with identity. Much modern advice tells young people to "figure out who you are" and then build a life that expresses that identity. In practice, this often devolves into constructing a brand. They decide they are an entrepreneur, an activist, an artist, an investor, a "next-gen leader," and then try to live up to the label. Without the three circles underneath, their pursuit is a costume. Authentic identity emerges from the cycle of building, receiving feedback, and contributing to others. Viktor Frankl observed that "happiness cannot be pursued; it must ensue."[4] In other words, you don't start *first* by deciding to be happy or having an identity. These result from your effort. "What is called self-actualization," he wrote, "is not an attainable aim at all, for the simple reason that the more one would strive for it, the more he would miss it. In other words, self-actualization is possible only as a side-effect of self-transcendence," or in other words, "a meaning to fulfill."[5]

Meaning is not something you can hand your children the way you might hand them keys or a diploma. You can't bequeath it to them. But you can shape the environment that makes it more or less likely they will find it. You can tell stories—like Frankl's and Vidor's—that frame struggle as part of the process. (More on this in the next chapter.) You can watch for the early signs of overlap between what your children build, how reality responds, and who benefits. You can help them interpret those moments when they recognize something that felt like it mattered. And you can make it clear, by what you praise and what you are willing to fund, that your family measures a life not by how easy it is, but by how much good it does.

Meaning as Gravity

Meaning also acts as a buffer for your children against the currents swirling around them. A teenager who has discovered that they love teaching younger children to swim and has seen those children come alive in the process will be more likely to ignore online fads that promise quick status. A young adult who has found satisfaction in building a small business is less likely to be impressed by peers who only perform wealth on social media. Their life has feedback and contribution baked into it. They know what it feels like when effort matters. That experience is hard to dislodge.

This brings us to the second framework: the relationship between meaning and comfort.

If you imagine a horizontal line, with maximum comfort on one end and maximum meaning on the other, most of modern life is arranged to keep people as far toward the comfort side as possible (see figure 9). The promise is as consistent as it is captive: less friction, fewer inconveniences, more ease. Faster shipping. Softer landings. Frictionless onboarding. For affluent families, that promise extends everywhere—education, health care, travel, household management, and even parenting. The more resources you have, the easier it is to keep sliding toward the comfort-heavy end of the line.

THE MEANING VS. COMFORT CONTINUUM

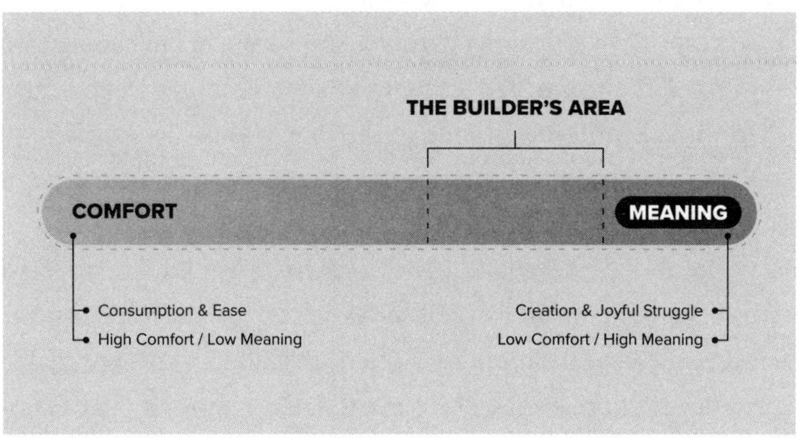

Figure 9

The problem is that meaning and comfort do not increase together; they operate, more often, as trade-offs. The more you aim your life at avoiding discomfort, the less room there is for meaningful struggle.

Builders intuitively know this. They are willing to accept a lower level of comfort in exchange for the chance to create something they care about.

On the comfort-max side, decisions revolve around what feels safe or pleasant right now. Jobs are chosen for salary and prestige first, fit and mission second. Free time gets filled with entertainment. Hard conversations get postponed. New ventures are avoided unless the odds of success seem very high and the cost of failure very low. Parents in this zone instinctively shield children from pain: They smooth social bumps, fight with teachers, and rush in to fix relationships or schedules the moment tension appears.

The availability of a short-term result—a dopamine hit—certainly makes this tempting. There are fewer tears, fewer arguments, fewer moments of anxiety. In the long term, though, a life lived this way tends toward numbness. Without repeated experiences of pushing through something hard because it matters, people lose track of what they are capable of. The inner narrative shifts from "I can handle hard things when they count" to "I should avoid hard things when I can."

On the meaning-heavy side of the line, choices look different. People still value rest and pleasure, but these are seen as fuel stops, not destinations. The central question is not "What will be easiest or most enjoyable?" but "What will be worth it?" Work is chosen at least in part because of the problems it solves and the people it serves—the value it creates and the meaning it offers us. Children are expected to experience friction, even when parents could remove it. Hard conversations are approached rather than endlessly deferred. The family assumes that some degree of suffering is healthy and welcome if it is attached to something bigger than comfort.

A builder's life sits closer to this side. That does not mean a builder seeks pain for its own sake; masochism is not meaning. It does mean they expect any worthwhile pursuit to involve sacrifice. Time, status, convenience, ego—something will be spent. As the renowned economist Thomas Sowell said, "There are no solutions; there are only trade-offs."[6] When the pursuit is rooted in the three circles of meaning, those sacrifices feel like a fair trade. They hurt in the moment and make sense in the long run. We accept sometimes feeling like hell, knowing that we are on the path to heaven.

Recalibrating Comfort

This obviously has implications for how you use comfort in your home. If every child's request is met with accommodation, if every inconvenient task is given to staff, if every difficult situation is medicated or scheduled away, you are quietly nudging your family toward the comfort end of the continuum. Letting kids quit a sport, club, or instrument the moment it stops being fun; paying professionals for every household job so they never have to scrub, mow, or fix anything; allowing them to skip any social setting that feels awkward or unfamiliar; and bailing them out of every financial mistake so they never feel the loss—all of these send the same message. You should not be surprised if your children later show little interest in spending significant time on a project that does not deliver quick emotional rewards. You have trained them, without saying a word, that comfort is the higher good.

Recalibrating this does not mean swinging to the other extreme. Rest matters. Joy matters. Beauty matters. A family that never relaxes or plays will burn itself out just as surely as a family that never does anything hard. The aim is balance tilted toward meaning: enough comfort to recover and bond, not so much that nobody ever needs to struggle.

Meaning built on these terms is the foundation of internal sovereignty—an inner authority over your own life, steering it based on convictions rather than noise. Without it, people are carried along by whatever external forces are loudest. With it, they can resist those forces when they conflict with the life they are trying to build.

Consider a young adult who has never developed a clear sense of their purpose. They have a little talent and intelligence but little understanding of or experience pursuing meaning. When a trend, ideology, or community promises belonging, validation, and an easy story about who they are, it is extremely hard to say no. Why would they? They have nothing equally strong to say yes to.

Now consider a young adult who, by their early twenties, has already spent several years inside the meaning sweet spot. They have run projects that mattered to them, handled the sting of failure, enjoyed the satisfaction of impact, and seen the difference between hollow praise and earned respect. When a recruiter dangles a seductive but soul-destroying job opportunity, or when well-meaning relatives urge them to "stop working so hard and just enjoy life" now that they have a trust behind them, or when a family advisor suggests they scale back their own venture and live off distributions instead, they still feel the pull of those easier paths. But they also know, in their bones, what it feels like to be fully engaged in something that stretches them and offers meaning. That memory provides them with a benchmark against which to measure.

That steadiness is a simple consequence of having a "why" that is stronger than the passing currents around you. Meaning gives a person their own gravity. It does the same for a family. When a family shares a common understanding of the purposes of its wealth and time, the offers and expectations of the world lose some of their pull. You may still send your children to elite schools, still work with sophisticated institutions, still live in relative comfort. But you do so as someone steering, not someone being steered. You do so with intention, ensuring that along the way you design enough struggle (see chapter 9) to ensure your children don't become intoxicated and incapacitated by the comforts they enjoy.

Helping your children move toward that kind of meaning requires giving them chances to step into the overlap of value creation, feedback, and contribution often enough that they start to recognize the feeling. It requires letting them see you make choices that favor meaning over comfort in your own life, and telling the truth about those trade-offs. You do not have to get this perfect. You only have to move the family's default setting. Right now, for many affluent households, the dial is turned significantly toward comfort. Automatic upgrades. Automatic outsourcing. Automatic insulation. If you begin to turn that dial even modestly toward meaning—by funding experiments instead of only luxuries, by letting kids struggle through real responsibilities, by talking openly about what you are building and for whom—you change the ambient story.

Over time, that story becomes the culture your heirs inherit. Not just "we have money," but "in this family, we do hard things that matter. We build. We serve. We pay attention to what works. We care about who is on the other side of our choices." That culture is the true inheritance. It is also the only thing that can keep your stored energy from dissolving into drift.

Principles

1. **The true inheritance is not capital but culture—identity, purpose, value creation.** What your children really inherit from you is not the size of the balance sheet, but the story your family lives by: who we are, what we're for, and how we create value for others. A strong, intentional culture quietly teaches them which kinds of effort matter, how to handle freedom, and what it means to be a builder instead of a beneficiary. Capital, without that culture, merely changes their lifestyle; culture, with or without capital, shapes their lives.

2. **Meaning gives direction to wealth; without it, wealth becomes drift.** Money is stored energy, and meaning is the map that tells it where to go. When your family has a clear sense of purpose, wealth becomes a means of building skills, solving problems, and serving people. When that purpose is missing, the same wealth ends up chasing comfort, status, and distraction, leaving your children with more options and less sense of why any of them matter.

Application Examples

These ideas matter most when translated from concept to concrete action. Below is a sampling of age-appropriate prompts to guide you with your children or grandchildren.

Get the full list at WealthTrapBook.com/list.

- **Ages 5–8**
  When you ask them to help, briefly connect it to meaning: "We clean up because we respect our home" or "We help with dinner so everyone can eat together." This teaches that even mundane tasks are part of a larger story they can come to understand.

- **Ages 9–12**
  Connect something they love to someone they can help. If they love art, help them design posters for a school event or cards for a nursing home. If they love tech, have them set up devices for grandparents or help a teacher with classroom tech. Use the pattern: "You like X. Here's how X can help someone."

- **Ages 13–17**
  When you see all three circles of meaning line up for them—what they built, the feedback they got, who they helped—be sure to articulate it. For example, "You worked hard on that,

people showed up, and they clearly got something out of it. That's the kind of thing you're good at." These moments serve as anchor points for how they see themselves.

- **Ages 18–25**

  If they have some flexibility, suggest six to twelve months for a deliberate experiment: starting something, apprenticing in a mission-driven role, or building a portfolio around a problem they care about. Help them outline what they want to build, who it's for, and how they'll know if it's going somewhere.

CHAPTER 5

From Preservation to Creation

On her twenty-first birthday, Kate Gardner expected a nice breakfast with her parents and maybe a small, symbolic step into adulthood. She was a junior at Princeton, thinking about exams and friendships and the usual questions of a young adult who knew her family was comfortably, even conspicuously, well off. Her father and uncle had founded a high-profile financial media firm; she'd grown up in a large house, traveling on very nice vacations, and she'd heard vague references to accounts that would one day be hers. Kate assumed that meant a generous cushion—a few hundred thousand dollars, perhaps—that might help with grad school or a down payment someday.

Over a wholesome meal, her parents told her that the investment account her father had held since she was born was now fully in her name. The number was not a few hundred thousand. It was a few million.

The air went out of the room. She remembers being shocked, then in awe, then oddly alone. On paper, nothing material had changed; the money had already existed in some sense. But authority had shifted. The decisions were now hers. "I think my body processed what happened to me as a trauma of sorts," she told us.[1] In the months that followed, she found herself carrying a new, invisible weight: "Some guilt, some questions of why I have this and people who need it way more than me don't, and some shame and feeling like I'm a misfit because of this wealth."

Becoming a builder is conceptual for some; in Kate's lineage, it's literal. Her great-grandfather built up and then sold an extremely successful construction-tool company, which to this day helps contractors and do-it-yourselfers turn raw materials into structures. Her father and uncle took the portfolios they had inherited as young men, learned to invest, and built a global firm that helped ordinary people grow their wealth. Generations of builders had produced the capital that now sat before Kate. The question was whether she would become a builder herself or retreat into a life of careful preservation.

Importantly, Kate did not receive this windfall in a vacuum. By the time the account turned over, she had already spent years cultivating character and faith. She describes her younger self as having "full-time ministry energy" even before she owned a stock. She wanted to live a life of service, to spread virtue, to align her days with something larger than herself. That foundation kept her from self-destruction. She did not run to the nearest dealership or private jet broker. She mostly did nothing with the money for two years.

Doing nothing, however, is still a choice. As she moved through her twenties, Kate realized the inheritance had changed more than her brokerage statement. It had altered the structure of her life. Her friends graduated into jobs they needed to live. She realized she might never need a paycheck in the same way. Money had shifted her from the realm of necessity into the realm of possibility. That shift brought freedom, but it also brought a question that felt as heavy as any obligation: *What is all this for?*

She wrestled with that question, and over time began to treat the wealth not as a dragon to guard but as energy she was responsible for directing. Years later, she coauthored a book, *Becoming Ascendants*, about moving from being a descendant of a successful family to becoming an ascendant—someone who integrates their inheritance into a purposeful life (or, in our words, becomes a builder).

Kate's story illustrates the central tension of this chapter. Wealth that is treated primarily as something to preserve eventually turns in on itself. Wealth that is treated as fuel for continued creation can renew a family's purpose across generations. Put differently, the survival of capital depends less on spreadsheets and safe withdrawal rates than on whether each generation is willing to keep building. To see why, it helps to zoom out beyond finance and consider how living systems work.

The Inevitability of Entropy

In ecology, entropy is the default. Left alone, everything drifts toward disorder. Bodies age. Buildings crumble. Forests, if not periodically renewed by fresh growth and even by fire, choke on deadwood. The only force that counters this drift is ongoing creative effort—energy poured into maintenance, adaptation, and new growth.

Vaclav Havel, a leading critic of the Czechoslovak communist regime, once wrote, "Just as the constant increase of entropy is the basic law of the universe, so it is the basic law of life to be ever more highly structured and to struggle against entropy."[2] (He would know—communism is an entropic accelerant across political and market institutions.) In plain terms, the universe is always pushing toward decay; the only way to resist is to build. That is why builders are best positioned to avoid the shirtsleeves-to-shirtsleeves outcome that befalls so many families.

Ecologists have distilled a simple rule: An organism survives only if its rate of adaptation keeps pace with, or exceeds, the rate of change in its environment. The world moves. Conditions shift. The species that treats its current state as permanent and optimizes purely for efficiency eventually gets blindsided by a change it did not see coming. The species that keeps experimenting and adapting, even when things are going well, has a far better chance of staying alive.

Families are not plants or animals, but they are systems embedded in changing environments—cultures, markets, technologies, and regulations. The same rule applies. A founding generation creates something of value that generates wealth. That act of creation requires adaptation. It forces them to develop new skills and habits, to solve real problems, and to read the landscape and respond.

Descendants, like Kate, inherit what was built. At that moment, a fork appears. One path is preservation: treat the assets as fragile relics and protect them at all costs. The other path sees wealth as stored energy—a platform to build what comes next. The first path feels safer. The second path is the only one that actually preserves anything over time. Preservation without ongoing creation produces fragility and accelerates entropy. Wealth survives only when purpose expands and creation continues. Builders win in the long run, every time.

It is important to be precise here. The argument is not that preservation is bad; defense and caution have their place. Legal structures, tax planning, basic prudence, and more—they all matter. The problem arises when preservation becomes the primary mission or the main filter for decision-making. When that happens, the family unconsciously shifts from tending a living garden to building a taller fence around whatever is growing today. Eventually, the garden withers, no matter how high the fence. The garden's ultimate preservation is a by-product of its ongoing growth and adaptation.

The message isn't to neglect or kill the existing value creation machine, but to use the surplus value it generates to create the next value creation machine. In this regard, true stewardship looks like disruption. Rather than preservation, future generations should be empowered to disrupt what already exists, because if they don't, the environment (i.e., the market) surely will. Better to be the disrupter than the disrupted.

Vicious and Virtuous Cycles

We can picture this shift through the New Paradigms model (see figure 10). On one side is a vicious cycle of preservation, consumption, and decay. On the other is a virtuous cycle of creation, empowerment, and compounding.

NEW PARADIGMS MODEL

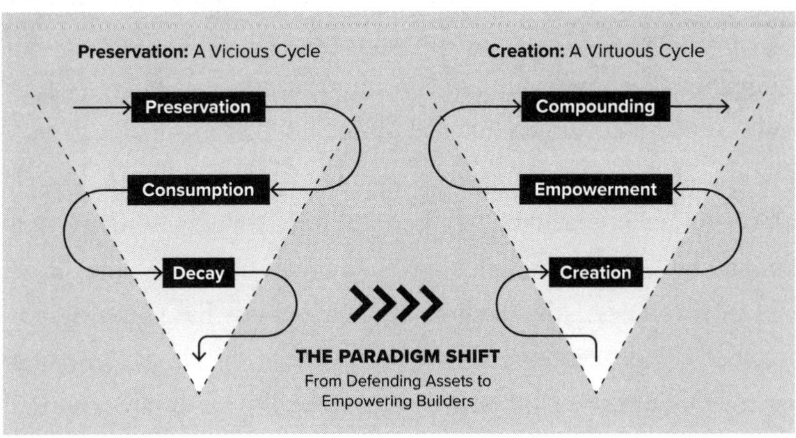

Figure 10

The vicious cycle begins when preservation becomes the primary objective. The family office, the trustees, and sometimes the matriarch or patriarch themselves center on one fear: Do not be the one who loses the wealth they created. Investment policies drift toward safety. Governance structures tighten. Risk gets framed as the enemy rather than as a necessary teacher and opportunity for growth. Young adults, as you might imagine, pick up the subtext quickly: The highest virtue here is not courage or creativity, but caution. And through the lens of "risk management," future generations internalize a future for themselves in which failure is not tolerated and must be avoided at all costs. So why try anything at all?

Energy has to go somewhere, though. When no one is building, the system still has to move. That is where consumption slides in. If you are not using capital to create new value, you will eventually use it to upgrade lifestyle. Said differently, if you are not moving toward a future that you believe in, you might as well make the present more comfortable and appealing. The upgrades may be tasteful—houses in better neighborhoods, more interesting trips, more convenient services—but over time the family starts to spend more time enjoying what exists than expanding what is possible. Philanthropy in this mode often becomes a kind of consumption too: gala tickets, named buildings, and donations that feel more like social dues than genuine attempts to solve problems and make the future a better place. The subconscious implication: We have arrived; there is nowhere to go from here.

Decay follows. Skills atrophy because nobody has to build under pressure. (This vicious cycle, if it's not yet obvious, is the process by which "spoiled brats" and stereotypical "trust fund kids" are produced; value creation is the antidote to value consumption.) Younger family members struggle to see where they fit, since all the interesting problems have already been solved before they arrived. Legitimacy erodes: Employees, advisors, and even the heirs themselves begin to see the structure as a relic rather than a living enterprise. Eventually, cohesion cracks because there is no shared mission beyond merely maintaining and enjoying the assets under management.

The virtuous cycle looks very different. It starts with creation as an ongoing practice. Each generation is expected to build something—not necessarily in the same industry or format, but with the same spirit of value creation. Capital is seen as fuel for experiments (which we'll dig into in chapter 10) rather than a relic to be hidden in a vault. Mistakes are treated as tuition, not disgrace.

This creation mindset naturally fosters empowerment. Instead of telling the next generation, "Don't mess this up," parents and grandparents say, "What are you going to build, and how can we empower you?" That empowerment might be financial, but it also includes introductions, mentoring, and the freedom to design a path that fits their meaning. The human capital becomes the primary focus: skills, character, and networks. Financial capital is seen for what it should always be: stored energy to fuel experimentation in value creation, developing human capital as a by-product of the process.

From there, compounding occurs across multiple axes. Financial returns may grow as new ventures succeed, but the more important compounding happens in capability and purpose. The family's answer to Kate's question—*What is all this for?*—grows, not shrinks. One generation might say, "We build tools that make others' work easier" (construction tool company). The next might say, "We help ordinary people invest wisely" (financial media business). A later generation might say, "We exist to encourage and equip inheritors to live lives of service and impact" (Kate's book, *Becoming Ascendants*). The more value you create, the more the impact compounds.

Without this kind of ongoing creation, even well-designed preservation strategies eventually fail. You can see a version of this in the FIRE movement—financial independence, retire early—which has become something of a secular religion in certain corners of the internet. At its core, FIRE is about building up a nest egg large enough that you can withdraw a small percentage each year, usually around 4 percent, and never have to work again. The math behind the "safe withdrawal rate" is carefully drawn from decades of market data. In that narrow sense, it is rational.

But after hundreds of hours spent reading through the various FIRE forums on Reddit and elsewhere, I can clearly see what often sits beneath the spreadsheets. There are success stories, of course: people who left jobs that were crushing their health, who now spend more time with family and do work they actually care about. There are also a vast number of posts from people who hit their number, walked away, and then realized they had quietly exited the game of life.

They did what the formulas said. They optimized their expenses, saved aggressively, invested wisely, and reached a point where their investment accounts could theoretically support them for the rest of their lives. Then they woke up a few years into "freedom" and noticed they had no story. Their days were filled with small pleasures—trips, hobbies, perhaps a little volunteering—but little that felt like creation. Some confess that their marriages strained as one spouse kept working and the other drifted. Others admit they lie to friends about what they do because they feel embarrassed admitting the truth. A few go back to work, not for the money, but for the meaning.

This is preservation mode in personal finance form. Everything is tuned to maintain a certain lifestyle with as little risk as possible. There is no slack for new ventures, for stepping into a problem that matters, for taking on responsibility that does not have a tidy financial return. On paper, it looks efficient. In life, it often feels hollow—void of meaning.

Families can fall into the same pattern on a larger scale. An estate plan is drawn up to keep the principal intact and to drip out carefully calibrated distributions. The family office is evaluated primarily on whether the portfolio stays within a specified volatility band and on minimizing taxes. Trustees are instructed that their job is to "preserve and protect." The implicit message to the next generation is clear: The story is already written; your task is to make sure the book doesn't get lost or destroyed.

To be clear, there is value in not spending recklessly and in guarding against obvious threats. But if the entire system is built around a safe-withdrawal-rate mentality—whether explicit or not—there is little room for the kind of creation that keeps purpose alive and empowers the next generation. No one is encouraged to swing for something that might fail. No one is invited to reconsider what the family is for in light of a changing world. The result is the financial equivalent of an early retirement to comfort: decades of existence, but very little life.

The alternative is neither reckless speculation nor perpetual hustle. It is a choice to keep creation at the center of the family's operating system (which we'll discuss in chapter 8). That choice requires slack: extra room in the schedule, and extra funds and patience for messy experiments. It requires accepting that some capital, when deployed in people and new ideas, will not return in familiar financial form. It may return as capacity, resilience, and stories instead. It may yield far more human capital than financial. And that's good. That's the point. Human capital is an upstream multiplier. Money compounds; capability and culture compound the compounding.

Slack's Hidden Strength

Imagine your family system as a spring. It carries weight—capital, commitments, and obligations—and when things are working, that weight is held in tension. The operative question is how tightly you choose to compress it. The temptation, especially for wealth creators who have succeeded in business, is to keep compressing until the spring fits perfectly under today's load. Every dollar is allocated. Every seat is filled. Every hour is scheduled. Things are neatly planned and predictable. From the outside, it all looks impressively efficient. Nothing is wasted.

The problem is that human beings aren't widgets, and life rarely respects static designs. Markets wobble, laws change, health fails, and revolutions in technology arrive. Children marry people you did not expect or move in directions you did not anticipate. A system tuned tightly to the present—or to your present perspective and preferences—has nowhere to go when things shift. The spring bottoms out. There is no give left. The structure breaks.

This is what the Value of Slack framework shows (see figure 11). In preservation mode, the spring is fully compressed under the current load—no play left, everything tuned to hold exactly what exists today. It looks tight and disciplined (no wasted space!), but any additional pressure has nowhere to go. In creation mode, the spring carries weight yet still has room to move. There is a deliberate margin built into the system. That slack is what lets a family absorb shocks, adjust to change, and lean into new opportunities without destroying what previous generations worked so hard to build.

Preservation mode treats slack as waste. Efficiency and performance are judged in terms of basis points—hundredths of a single percentage point. In the beginning, systems are efficient. Over time, systems calcify, administrative burdens grow, and the team ossifies. The family office stops hiring talent or considering innovation because there is no additional bandwidth to tolerate the mental load of adaptation. The human capital needs of the family become neglected, and the administrative needs of the financial capital are the only needs being served. In the extreme, especially during tax season, it appears that the office exists to serve the IRS rather than to serve the family, or even its financial capital.

THE VALUE OF SLACK

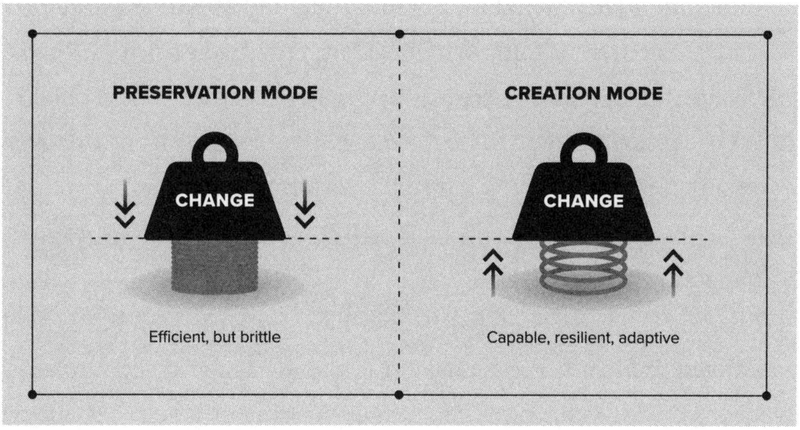

Figure 11

In the short term, this approach produces tidy reports. Expenses are controlled, and performance appears stable. The spring holds (while things are predictable, that is). Then something unexpected leans on the system—a lawsuit, a health crisis, a market disruption, a family rift, or other—and there is nowhere left to compress. Because there is no slack, the new load is not absorbed; it is transmitted as breakage. Relationships fracture. Assets must be liquidated under pressure. People melt down in ways that look sudden but were actually years in the making.

Creation mode takes the opposite view. Instead of cranking a weak spring tighter, you put energy into thickening the metal and adding coils. More than mere empty space, slack is unused capacity you have deliberately built. A stronger spring with additional coils more than simply survives the current load with breathing room—it can actually push back against it, lifting and carrying more than before. In family terms, creation mode builds an upward force: The more you invest in capability, the more weight your system can bear without buckling.

In a fully loaded system, preservation mode can manage only priorities that are both important and urgent. And priorities that are important, but not urgent, are pushed off in perpetuity. The problem is that those priorities tend to be *the most impactful drivers of long-term value creation*. Building slack into the system creates an upward force that enables focus on strategy, relationships, development, experimentation, and rapid adaptation.

Practically, that upward force looks like human capital that exceeds today's requirements. People have skills beyond their current roles, so they can step into new problems and opportunities when they appear. Relationships extend beyond what is immediately useful, so there is somewhere to turn when you need perspective or help. Capital is set aside for learning and experiments, not only for protection. Over time, these "extra coils" mean your family can take on harder challenges—larger ventures, bolder philanthropy, more complex risks—because the spring is strong enough to handle them. Creation doesn't just keep the structure from breaking; it steadily raises what your family is capable of carrying.

A family in creation mode might decide, for example, that a certain percentage of its annual distributions will fund next-gen experiments: a child's first small business, an apprenticeship in a field nobody in the family knows, a sabbatical project for a mid-career parent, or a high-risk philanthropic initiative. That money may or may not beat the market in financial terms, but it will almost certainly add slack to the system: new skills, new contacts, new stories, and new ways of thinking about what the family is capable of. Again, this form of derivative value creation positions individuals and the human capital system to be upstream multipliers of direct value creation.

In a very real sense, human capital is the slack that keeps financial capital alive. In preservation mode, you focus on protecting the money and neglect the people, so the portfolio has no one strong enough to adapt it when conditions inevitably change. In creation mode, you invest first in builders—their skills, judgment, and willingness to experiment—and they become the extra coils in the spring that allow the family's financial capital to absorb shocks, find new uses, and keep growing instead of slowly bleeding out. In short, slack is what turns pressure into progress instead of panic.

Freedom with a Frame

All of this leads to a deeper question: What, exactly, are you trying to preserve?

Most families answer by focusing on their financial assets, but that answer is too narrow. A portfolio is a tool, not a purpose, and cannot justify its own existence. Nobody hoards batteries for the sake of it; the point of acquiring energy is to apply it toward something productive. The thing worth preserving is *the family's ability to create new value in the world*—its capacity to write new chapters that are worth reading.

That means the goal is not simply to defend assets but to empower builders. Empowering builders becomes the lens through which decisions—especially financial ones—are to be made.

Every generation of children needs the freedom to build something new, but those children also need a frame that connects their efforts to a larger story.

The worst version of this is a frozen mission statement from the wealth creator. The world moves too fast for that. Markets, technologies, and social norms that made sense in one decade may be irrelevant or even harmful two generations later. A family that insists every descendant must faithfully execute the vision and ideals of those who first built the family's financial capital is asking to become a museum piece—preserved, perhaps, but trapped.

The frame is better understood as a set of commitments about how the family approaches creation. For example:

- We use our freedom to create value, not just to consume.
- We measure ourselves by the problems we solve and the people we serve, not by the things we own.
- We expect each generation to reinterpret "what we are for" in light of the world they are actually living in, but we expect them to do so from a builder's posture, not from a beneficiary's lounge.
- We strive to continually deepen our understanding of "why we exist" and of the future we are responsible for.

You might even express this as an invitation (or dare!) to the next generation: *Figure out how to kill us before someone else does*. The next generation ought to be a disrupter, not just a caretaker. That might mean expanding into new lines of business when it becomes clear the industry is evolving or in decline. It might mean shifting the family's philanthropic center of gravity to a different geography or cause. It might mean repurposing existing capabilities, brands, or capital into something unrecognizable to the founder—but that honors the founder's spirit and meaning more than rigid preservation ever could.

Families should see themselves not as stewards of assets, but as stewards of a story. If you consider assets to be ink and paper, then the story is what gets written with them. Instead of preserving the text of the first chapter at all costs, the aim is to ensure that there is no final chapter—that each generation picks up the pen and keeps writing.

That requires a different way of thinking about risk. In a preservation paradigm, the only legitimate risk is losing money or reputation. Everything else is subordinated to that fear. In a creation paradigm, the greater risk is failing to grow new builders. Losing some capital on the way to forming a capable, purposeful descendant is an acceptable trade. It should be the reason we create financial capital in the first place.

Intergenerational Storytelling

Preservation mode looks backward. It tries to embalm a particular moment in a family's history and hold it in place. Creation mode faces forward. It treats the past as prologue to something even better in the future. Historian Thomas Babington Macaulay once observed that "a people which takes no pride in the noble achievements of remote ancestors will never achieve anything worthy to be remembered with pride by remote descendants."[3] The converse is also true: When you are proud only of what is behind you, and add nothing of your own, the line eventually goes dim. Ongoing creation is what keeps the story bright enough for future generations to see and carry. We honor the builders who came before us by continuing their calling of building the future.

Your family's true legacy is the ongoing ability to write new chapters that are worth reading. That is why so many of the metaphors we reach for when talking about long-term thinking involve time and selflessness: planting trees whose shade you will never sit under; building cathedrals that will not be finished in your lifetime; making your present better by making your future bigger. When you orient around creating value that will outlive you, your own choices in the here and now start to look different. You begin to ask not only *What do I want?* but, *What am I building today that my grandchildren's grandchildren might be grateful for?*

Taylor experienced this shift when he started digging into his own family's history. He was aware that the family was descended from the Adamses of colonial fame and he knew, vaguely, that he had other interesting remote ancestors—like King Vidor, the renowned film director, and Commodore Morgan Adams Sr., a businessman and yachtsman who became the first person to pay a toll to the US government for use of the newly constructed Panama Canal. But when he began researching their lives in detail, reaching out to archives and reconstructing their stories, something unexpected happened. Their stories energized him. He describes it as almost a spiritual experience, a sense of borrowed courage and momentum that created a connection to some form of ancestral energy. In biblical language, it felt like what the prophet Malachi described: the hearts of the fathers turning to the children and the hearts of the children to the fathers.[4] Honoring what they had built did not trap him in nostalgia; it pushed him to ask whether his own life would be a chapter worthy of the same book. Taylor saw builders in his ancestry and became increasingly motivated to become one himself.

That same dynamic is available to you. For some families, looking back reveals a line of builders whose stories are simply waiting to be recovered and retold. For others, the past is marked more by absence, damage, or misuse of capital—but the reality is that you exist today and your line is flourishing, so your remote ancestors must have done something right; at a minimum, they survived! In those cases where meaningful stories are not accessible, the task is to consciously write a different kind of chapter. Creation mode makes room for both. It calls you to live a life that your descendants could point to with pride and to tell enough of that story, and enough of the stories that came before, that your descendants know they are part of something larger than their own existence. And it invites you to give your descendants slack—time, capital, and trust—so they can add their own scenes, in their own ways, to that larger narrative.

This, ultimately, is why creation matters so much more than preservation, and why human capital has to sit at the center of any serious generational plan. Financial capital can be frozen, hoarded, or dripped out according to formulas, but that does not keep it alive. Only builders do that. When you keep producing people who know how to read changing conditions, how to solve problems, how to create value for others, and how to carry a story forward, your wealth—whatever its numeric size—retains a reason to exist. It serves freedom instead of eroding it. It becomes a tool for meaning instead of a cushion for drift.

Principles

1. **Preservation without creation produces fragility and accelerates entropy.** When a family treats its main job as avoiding financial losses, then skills atrophy, slack disappears, and the system becomes brittle. It may look efficient for a while, but without new builders, new ideas, and new value being created, the first real shock exposes how hollow everything has become. Trying to freeze a moment in time doesn't keep it alive; it speeds up its own decay.
2. **Wealth survives only when purpose expands.** Instead of guarding capital, keep it healthy by using it in service of a growing mission. Each generation has to widen the family's answer to *what is all this for?* and build something of its own, or the money eventually loses its reason to exist and drifts into consumption and conflict. When purpose grows, the people grow—and the wealth has a meaningful job to do instead of just sitting there.

Application Examples

These ideas matter most when translated from concept to concrete action. Below is a sampling of age-appropriate prompts to guide you with your children or grandchildren.

Get the full list at WealthTrapBook.com/list.

- **Ages 5–8**
  At bedtime, swap in a few stories about ancestors who created something. Emphasize what that act of building meant for

their life, and what it means for yours. Ask your child, "What do you think they would be proud of you building one day?"

- **Ages 9–12**
  Invite them to disrupt a small family routine or tradition to replace it with something they think could improve it. Let them propose an alternative and test it a few times (e.g., a family meeting format, chore system, or game night). This shows that systems aren't sacred and can be redesigned.
- **Ages 13–17**
  Give them a creation budget, not just spending money. Alongside any allowance or job income, set aside a small "creation budget" that they can only use to launch or improve something: a small business, online project, workshop, event, or prototype. Require a simple one-page pitch and a short postmortem.
- **Ages 18–25**
  Bring them into the discussion of preservation versus creation. Show them, at a high level, the family's balance sheet and estate structure. Ask, "Where do you see us overoptimizing for preservation? Where should we be creating instead?" Take at least one of their ideas seriously enough to act on.

CHAPTER 6

The Directionality of Family Purpose

Most Americans haven't read the Declaration of Independence in years, if ever. They couldn't quote more than a sentence or two from the Constitution—if even that—if pressed. They have only the vaguest sense of what the *Federalist Papers* argued or why the Bill of Rights was structured the way it was. And yet the vast majority of them have a high regard for these documents and know, instinctively, what it means to be an American.

That knowledge comes from something deeper than memorizing documents—a cultural gravity that has shaped how Americans think about freedom, opportunity, and individual agency for a quarter of a millennium. The Founders did more than simply write laws; they established a directionality. They articulated a vision of who Americans were, who they could become, and the principles that would guide their journey. That vision has been interpreted and reinterpreted by every subsequent generation, amended over two dozen times, tested in war and social upheaval, yet it still exerts a pull strong enough that children born two and a half centuries later feel its influence and benefit from its creation without ever consciously studying it.

What the Founders did for a nation, you can do for your family. You can establish a directionality of purpose—not a rigid script to follow, but a cultural gravity that shapes how your posterity thinks about who they are, what they can build, and how they ought to show up in the world. The question isn't whether your family has a direction. Every family moves somewhere; people, like energy and money, flow. The question is whether that direction was designed with intention or whether you're drifting on currents you never chose and aren't even aware of.

Alignment Without Control

We previously explored how preservation without creation produces fragility and accelerates entropy. The same principle applies to family alignment itself. Families that try to align through control—mandating participation, prescribing acceptable careers, enforcing uniformity of belief and behavior, and so on—inevitably produce the opposite of what they intend. They breed resentment, stifle agency, and create the conditions for the very rebellion they fear. Parents who employ these tactics unwittingly become their own worst enemy.

Let's use a nautical metaphor to unpack this. Imagine a family that has accumulated significant wealth, and the patriarch decides that the best way to protect it is to put everyone on the same yacht. The supplies are plentiful—enough to last for generations, theoretically. But because no one needs to fish and provide for themselves, no one learns how. Because the patriarch acts as captain and has chosen a fixed destination, no one develops navigation skills. The family floats together, consuming whatever is available, until someone eventually notices the supplies are running low. By then, it's too late for rationing.

We might call this approach controlled collectivism, and it operates at the family level much like political collectivism operates at the societal level: mandatory participation, prescribed roles, and performative unity—governance structures that substitute obedience for meaning. It looks like legacy planning and feels like prudent stewardship. But underneath, it usually produces the exact outcomes the family was trying to prevent: dependency, resentment, and eventual fragmentation.

The alternative is a structure entirely different. Instead of a single yacht where everyone is stuck together, consuming shared supplies and forced to travel toward the same destination, picture an armada. Each family member—or each nuclear family unit—has their own vessel. They have the agency to wander, to explore, to chart their own course. But they all share a common heading. They're oriented toward the same infinite horizon. And because they know the armada's direction, even if they lose sight of the fleet for a season or choose for other reasons to pursue side quests, they can always find their way back. They're never truly lost because they know where everyone is heading.

A family aligned by direction can tolerate divergence—different careers, different geographies, different expressions of the family's values. A family aligned by control cannot tolerate growth, interpreting every deviation as a threat, every independent decision as a betrayal. And in doing so, it guarantees that the most capable, most entrepreneurial family members will eventually leave—either physically or emotionally—because the system has no room for them to become the version of themselves that offers the most meaning.

Control doesn't scale. It's limited by the bandwidth of those in charge and the boundaries of established governance. Influence, by contrast, can travel anywhere and everywhere. It can reach across generations, across geographies, across the boundaries of any formal structure. A family that builds alignment through shared direction rather than shared control creates something that can outlast any individual, any trust document, any family council. It creates a culture.

Culture as the Bridge

The eighteenth-century philosopher and statesman Edmund Burke described society as a contract—but not the kind most people imagine. He wrote that society is "a partnership not only between those who are living, but between those who are living, those who are dead, and those who are to be born."[1] Burke's insight applies cleanly to families. You are not just in partnership with your spouse, siblings, or children. You are in partnership with remote ancestors you've never seen and remote descendants you'll never meet. Assets and documents can move across that time span, but they do not carry meaning in and of themselves. Culture does. Capital transfers wealth. Culture transfers identity.

Culture, in this sense, is not a list of values in vinyl on the family room wall or printed on a page rarely read. It is, rather, a story enacted through behavior. It is the set of lived answers to questions like: *Who are we? What do we believe in? What do we do when things get hard? What do we do when things go well? What kind of people do we admire? What do we consider beneath us? Who do we believe we will become?* Your children or grandchildren are already absorbing those answers. When you say nothing, they still learn. Silence teaches too.

Researchers at Emory University discovered this effect in a simple way: They asked children twenty basic questions about their family history—where grandparents grew up, how parents met, whether anyone had ever faced something really hard, the story of their own birth—and then compared the answers with measures of emotional health. The kids who knew the most about their family's past had the strongest sense of control over their lives, higher self-esteem, and a clearer belief that their families functioned well.[2] The key wasn't a glossy "we've always been successful" tale or a permanent victim story, but what the researchers called an oscillating narrative: We've had ups and downs, we've built and lost and rebuilt, and we stick together through it. In short, children who grow up hearing honest, hopeful stories about their people develop what the study called an "intergenerational self"—a lived sense that they belong to something larger than themselves. Every time you tell those stories in your own family, you are not sharing trivia; you are quietly wiring a durable identity and a bias toward perseverance into the next generation.

The most enduring families understand that culture is the bridge between their ancestors' grit and their descendants' goals. Ancestors provide the origin story—the anchoring context. The present generation provides the interpretation: Here is what those stories mean to us now, in our circumstances. And descendants provide the next expression of that story, determining how those values will be lived moving forward. Culture is where that handoff either happens or fails.

This is one reason the "self-made" myth among first-generation wealth creators is so corrosive. It tempts founders to disconnect themselves from the people and stories that made their own rise possible. "We came from nothing" might feel emotionally true when you think about your parents' bank balances. But it erases the nonfinancial capital that shaped you: the teacher who believed in you, the grandparent who modeled work, the immigrants who crossed an ocean rather than accept stagnation, the unknown soldier who didn't die in a battle that your bloodline might otherwise have ended in. When you cultivate contempt or indifference for the past, you weaken your descendants' ability to draw strength from it. We all stand on the shoulders of giants.

These anchoring contexts can be either near or far. In Taylor's case, that's a connection to John Adams and the inspiring legacy he created;

it's also the architectural renderings he keeps hanging in his office of his grandfather's real estate development projects—not because they are masterpieces of design but because they remind him, at a glance, "You can just do things." (The same story is told by King Vidor's Oscar that sat on a shelf in his father's study when he was a boy.) These memorialized stories don't dictate Taylor's life path or purpose, but they do shape what feels natural and accessible. These stories transmit an unspoken expectation and a spiritual responsibility to pursue a calling and continue building. Once internalized, it becomes clear that the world itself is a museum of passion projects; what's better than to make a contribution?

My line looks different but works the same way. A trucker grandfather who pulled me into politics as a college student, exposing me to books and essays that taught me the power of ideas and the importance of boldly sharing truth. A grandmother who, with no relevant education or experience, wrote a history book. Her daughter—my mother—who wrote a dozen books and became a community builder and elected official. When I started writing (now with fifty-plus books to my name), engaging in the political process, and launching organizations of my own, I was not acting out of the blue. I was stepping into a pattern that had already been laid down. I had stories to inspire me and directionality that guided me. I had an "intergenerational self."

Your line has its own characters. Some of their stories are probably easy to tell and immediately inspiring. Others might be tangled up with pain, addiction, betrayal, or mental illness. Please note that that doesn't disqualify them. In fact, those complexities can often make them more useful. A sanitized myth is brittle. An honest story can convey discernment; by helping children see the good and the bad—and helping them echo the good and avoid the bad—we sincerely convey that humans are flawed and life is messy, but that we can still build on our legacy, no matter what it looks like.

What Directionality Looks Like

Family culture is one story, but many chapters. Each generation inherits a narrative it did not write. They then face a choice: deny it, ignore it, or engage it. When they engage, they have to decide which parts to carry forward, which parts to leave behind, and how to extend the story into new terrain. That work—selecting, editing, adding—is the essence of directionality of purpose at the family level. It's part of being one vessel in an armada, with flexibility to move in and out and change course where circumstances might dictate.

Directionality of purpose gives your family a simple narrative arc:

1. Who we were and where we came from.
2. Who we are and how we contribute.
3. Who do we believe we can become, and what does the world look like when we get there?

"Who we were and where we came from" is the anchoring context spanning at least two or three generations back—ideally, people who died before you were born. It's not about the financial story, but the character of the people who got you here. The immigrant who took a risk. The single mother who kept things afloat. The shop owner who treated people fairly. The farmer who held land through drought. The scientist who insisted on truth when it was unpopular. The warrior who fought in battle. If you don't know these stories yet, your first job is to dig. Ask older relatives. Read old letters. Look up obituaries. Explore websites like FamilySearch.org or Ancestry.com. Find a handful of concrete moments that serve as anchoring context. The stories are there; they happened. You just need to see if you can find them.

"Who we are and how we contribute" is your present culture as actually lived. Not the aspirational mission statement a consultant helped you draft, but the day-to-day pattern your kids are already experiencing. Do family members talk openly about money and meaning, or are such matters ignored or deferred to consultants to handle? Do people discuss mistakes as learning opportunities or as scandals? Does the family get animated when talking about problems to solve or status to maintain? When someone new marries in, what do they notice first? If you asked your children to finish the sentence, "In our family, we . . . ," what would they say without thinking? Most parents overestimate how clear their current culture is. One thing that can improve it? Setting up systems to reinforce what you value most. (Hang tight, we'll get there in chapter 8.)

"Who do we believe we can become, and what does the world look like when we get there?" is the forward vector. This is where many families either get grandiose or go silent. They either go straight to a singular lofty slogan or they avoid the question altogether because it feels presumptuous. The most helpful way to think about it is this: Given where we came from and where we are today, what kinds of futures do we feel called to create? Directionality of purpose is an aspirational narrative about contribution that has a linear throughline, anchored in ancestral context, moving through current beliefs and capabilities toward a future you believe in and aspire to contribute to.

This three-part arc is captured in the Directionality of Purpose framework (see figure 12). Picture your life—or your family's life—as a tall cylinder composed of a throughline connecting three instances of value reflections (from figure 3). The bottom band represents who you were and where you came from. The middle band is who you are and where you are today. The top band is who you believe you can become and what the world will look like when you get there. Every decision you make either reinforces or bends that thematic throughline. But which anchoring context should you choose? Which storyline? The good news is that you don't have to pick just one—and the more stories you collect, the better. When you genuinely explore the lives of your remote ancestors, you discover a seemingly inexhaustible source of anchoring context, each thread capable of weaving its way through your present and into a future you believe in. Generations pass, and new ones arrive, but the thematic throughlines of human life endure. Your only job is to become aware of your own personal connection to them.

DIRECTIONALITY OF PURPOSE

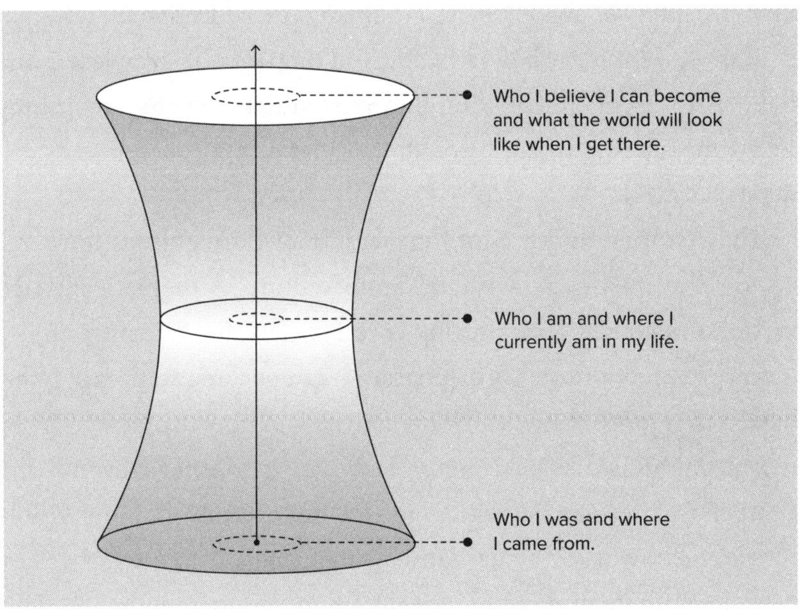

Figure 12

This is why a family's directionality of purpose is a collection of stories that, taken together, form a kind of thematic scaffolding—a structure future generations can use to make sense of their own lives and understand how their individual experiences fit into a larger context. That scaffolding is the foundation for meaning. When children and grandchildren absorb multigenerational throughlines through story, they begin—often without realizing it—to develop a dynamic, evolving sense of their own directionality of purpose. They grow more aware of who their people were, who they themselves are now, and, most importantly, who they believe they are capable of becoming. They feel less alone and less adrift, because the stories give them a sense of belonging and a precedent that says *keep moving*.

What makes this process so powerful is that it works in both directions across time, often invisibly. As someone's awareness and capacity for contribution grow, they may never fully recognize that their own directionality was shaped by internalizing the collective directionality of those who came before them. And they may be even less aware that the stories of contribution they are living today are establishing the anchoring context for throughlines that remote descendants will one day draw on.

These stories, and the multigenerational throughlines they create, are also the raw material of family culture. A thematically rich portfolio of stories transmitting core family values—contribution, adventure, creation, stewardship, care—can become so deeply internalized that those values show up naturally in how people live. They become embodied in behavior as each person journeys toward who they believe they can become. And when one family member visibly pursues their own self-actualization with purpose beyond themselves, it inspires others to do the same (more on this in chapter 11). This is the compounding force that establishes a family's directionality of purpose as the vector sum of each family member's own directionality. (Or, the armada.)

You can use this framework in a very simple way. Start in the past and jot a few words or names that capture your real origins: the town, the trade, the hardships, the key temperaments. What was life like then, and what value was being created? What meaning was experienced? Move to the present and write a brutally honest description of your current reality: how you actually live, what your days look like, what your children see. What value is reflecting back right now, and what does it look like? Then, for the future, describe—in plain language—the kind of person you intend to become and the kind of future chapters you want your descendants to inherit: the problems you want your family to be known for solving, the way you hope they will describe "what we're about."

Once the three bands are on paper, you can see the directional line you've been following so far. (Keep collecting those stories and their thematic throughlines!) In some families, the past is full of grit—immigrants, builders, teachers, people who took real risks—while the present reads like comfortable preservation: meetings, portfolio reviews, and an aversion to risk. The future, if it is contemplated at all, often shrinks to vague commitments to "keep it together" or "not screw this up." This framework makes that shrinkage visible. It shows that, unless creation reenters the picture, the line is thinning to stasis.

In other cases, the past and present bands look surprisingly similar. The family is still grinding the same way its grandparents did, but the future—what they believe they can become—has never been clearly envisioned. Everyone is busy. No one is steering. Here, the work is different: to lift the imagined future higher than the inherited present, to give children and grandchildren a horizon worth stretching toward rather than simply a lifestyle to maintain. Broaden the aperture of your future contribution landscape. Make your present better by making your future bigger.

The point of this exercise is to expose the direction you and your family are actually taking, so you can decide whether to keep or alter that vector. A teenager who sees this diagram sketched honestly for the family is no longer floating in abstraction. They can see: "This is where we came from. This is where we are. This is where we say we're going." They can then ask themselves whether their own choices—how they spend their time, what they study, how they treat work—are moving in that same general direction or quietly pulling the line in a different direction (or no direction at all). They can determine the direction their own vessel will take relative to the armada, but their multigenerational compass will influence their journey more than they know. It will establish the need for direction, and regardless of how dynamic and nonlinear it is, direction is better than idle drift.

The Family's Purpose Potential

Life, of course, is neither so fixed nor so simple that it can be fully represented as a straight line. Your agency allows you to flee the armada should you so choose, or make any number of deviations and detours. The arc of your children's lives can and will branch over time. Hence, the Purpose Potential framework (see figure 13).

Imagine your life as a node in the center. To the left are dozens of paths, each representing a possibility that once existed: different places you could have grown up, schools you might have attended, careers you might have chosen, people you might have married. Some of those paths were never realistic; most were closed by your own decisions. You didn't move to that country. You didn't pursue that opportunity. You didn't take that job. Whether wisely or not, those branches are now past.

To the right, running forward into the future, are the possibilities still open to you. Some are narrow and conservative; others are bolder. The key fact is that there are many. You have not been locked into a single track; your own directionality is dynamic, as is that of your children. At the same time, your current node—the life you've actually built—shapes what is realistically possible next. You cannot go back and relive your twenties. You can, however, choose a different direction from here. Your family's direction can shift and move toward a path with greater potential for purpose.

PURPOSE POTENTIAL FRAMEWORK

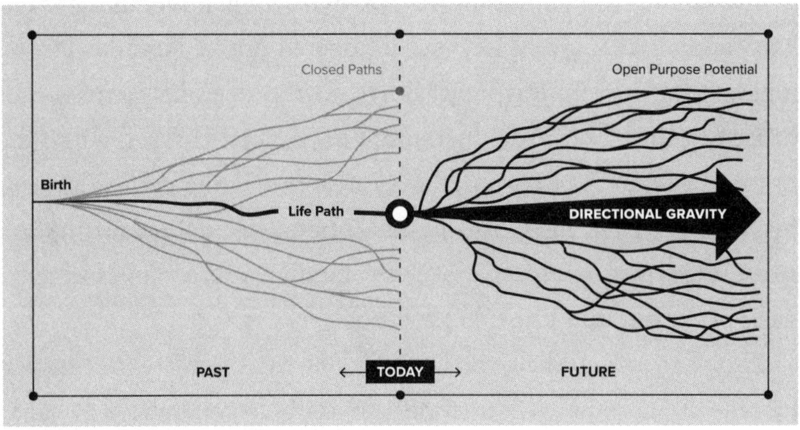

Figure 13

Purpose adds directional gravity and opens new pathways of opportunity. When you clarify what your life is for and what kind of person you're trying to become, the potential paths do not collapse into one, but they begin to cluster. Certain branches suddenly look out of character; others feel like natural extensions of your trajectory, and new ones appear. You still have agency. The point of purpose is not to turn your future into train tracks. The point is to tilt the entire field so that motion toward some futures feels more aligned than others.

The same is true at the family level. A founding generation makes choices—where to live, what industry to enter, which values to honor or ignore. Those choices open some branches for descendants and close others. An immigrant who comes to the United States on a one-way ticket closes off hundreds of paths in the country they left, but opens up a vast new tree of possibilities for their grandchildren. A founder who builds a respected local business opens doors of reputation, network, and knowledge that their heirs can walk through or ignore. Every act of value creation you encourage in your lifetime changes what will be realistically possible for heirs you will never meet.

Thomas Powell's story captures this dynamic in a very human way. His grandfather, a geologist who discovered one of Nevada's largest mines, moved his family from wealth to poverty in a single stroke—not through malice, but through a failure to prepare. He died without a transfer structure. The corporation's partners took the stock. Thomas's mother went from money to none. Thomas himself grew up poor, surrounded by the children of wealthy families whose names were on many of the buildings near Lake Tahoe.

Thomas's own node in the Purpose Potential tree began with that mix: the memory of a lost fortune, proximity to generational wealth, and a childhood of scarcity. When he later became financially successful, he could have swung hard toward preservation. He could have hoarded, silently enjoyed the life he never had as a child, and repeated his grandfather's mistake. Instead, he decided to continue building on a separate branch that offered more purpose.

Thomas shared an experience when his then–teenage daughter, Candace, asked what kind of car she would get at sixteen. When he indicated that one would not be provided, her retort was rather predictable given the environment in which she was being raised: "But we're rich!" Thomas's reply reset the trajectory: "*I'm* rich. You're poor. What kind of car you can buy is the kind of car you'll drive."[3]

That response, though humorous or flippant in some contexts, had directional intent for Thomas and his family. He had watched what happened to his young peers when they never had to do anything. He knew that if his children's tree of possibilities did not include learning to earn, decide, and fail, he would be building the same brittle branch he had seen break so many times. So he and his wife put their kids to work in the business at normal wages, required them to allocate their earnings—tithe, save, invest for a future venture, then spend—and even gave Candace a simple Excel sheet to track it all. When she wanted $100 jeans at fifteen, he had her calculate the post-tax, post-tithe hours it would cost. The math worked out to nearly three weeks of part-time work. She still chose to buy them. He let her. The point wasn't to block the purchase; it was to ensure the path she was choosing had visible trade-offs.

Years later, Candace still uses a version of that spreadsheet to manage her household finances. More importantly, she has a clear sense of what it means to be a Powell. Her children carry Powell as their middle name. When she talks about her family's direction, she doesn't start with money. She talks about resilience, problem-solving, creativity, and generosity—being "crafty" enough to figure things out and kind enough to help others while you do so. That is the cultural gravity she feels compelled to extend to her own kids.

Reorientation, Not Arrival

A pilot metaphor is useful here. No pilot flies a perfectly straight line from takeoff to landing. Wind pushes the aircraft off course. Weather systems require detours. Instruments drift. The pilot must continually reorient toward the destination, making small corrections as conditions change. A flight from New York to Los Angeles involves thousands of micro-adjustments. The plane is technically "off course" most of the time. And yet it lands where it intended to land.

Family direction works the same way. The horizon stays constant—a shared sense of purpose and identity, the armada's heading. But the specific expression of that purpose in each generation requires regular recalibration. Mission and values are not artifacts to be preserved under glass. They must be reiterated in conversation, integrated into decisions, and put into practice through behavior. This is how human capital compounds across generations: through reminders of family direction and constant, gentle reorientation toward the shared horizon.

A family that never revisits its direction isn't being loyal to its purpose; it's being lazy about it. The Constitution has been amended twenty-seven times—not because the Founders got it wrong, but because they were wise enough to build in a mechanism for adaptation. Your family's direction should carry the same humility. The anchoring context itself remains fixed in the sense that the past is the past—what happened, happened. But the reservoir of stories it contains is vast, and you can always reorient toward the particular threads most aligned with your current chapter of life. The present expression and future trajectory, then, are perpetually open to refinement. And in the very act of refining—of living, building, and choosing—you are creating new stories and new anchoring context that generations to come will draw on.

This leads to a crucial reframe. The conventional approach to family legacy puts all the attention on "preparing the next generation"—as if the older generation's job is to train, equip, and eventually hand off to their children. But that framing creates subtle problems. It places expectations on the children. It generates pressure. And pressure, especially pressure to fulfill someone else's vision, often triggers the very resistance parents are trying to avoid.

Instead of the older generation preparing the younger, picture the living generations *partnering together* to answer a different question: What are we building today that will empower generations three, five, ten from now—people we'll never meet—to pursue their own self-actualization in service of others? What stories can we coauthor now that will serve as cultural scaffolding for those who come long after us? Notice what changes when you shift to this frame. The focus shifts from the pressure and expectations placed on current children to a partnership in service toward future descendants, with a clear shared responsibility. We think less of what our kids might do to squander what we've built, and think more of what all of us—parents and children together—are building that will matter long after we're gone. That shift removes the adversarial dynamic that so often poisons conversations about family wealth. Everyone becomes a partner in a shared project rather than a participant in a high-stakes evaluation. We shift from inheritance and expectation to partnership and future-centric value creation.

That shift also does something unexpected to your relationship with time. When the horizon stretches to generations you will never meet, the pressure to judge outcomes in your own lifetime falls away. You will never know with certainty whether what you built "worked." You can only believe that it is *working*—directionally, incrementally, compoundingly. And that belief, paradoxically, is liberating. A hyperelongated time horizon encourages risk-taking, because no single decision in a single generation can be declared a final failure. It opens the door to derivative value creation and long-tail value capture—ideas and investments whose returns may not materialize for decades but whose potential is enormous. When the question shifts from "What can we accomplish before I die?" to "What can we set in motion that will still be compounding long after we're gone?" the entire landscape of possibilities changes. Bolder questions become natural. Larger bets become rational. The family stops optimizing for the quarter and starts building for the century.

There's something powerful about serving people you know you'll never meet. It removes the ego, the desire for recognition, and the temptation to control outcomes. It focuses attention on building systems and culture rather than managing individuals. The timeline extends. The grip loosens. The emphasis moves from preservation to creation, from control to influence.

And influence, unlike control, can scale infinitely. Control is bounded by the bandwidth of those in charge and the boundaries of the governance structure. You can't govern from the grave. But your influence can remain—and compound—long after your death. The stories you tell, the values you embody, the direction you establish: These can travel across generations without any active intervention on your part. That's what makes culture so much more powerful than compliance.

Directional Gravity

You are not inventing your family's purpose from scratch. Because of that anchoring context—the stories of who you were and where you came from—the purpose already exists. It's embedded in the patterns of who your ancestors were and how they showed up in the world. The work isn't invention; it's excavation. You're uncovering something that's been there all along, perhaps unarticulated, perhaps forgotten, but present in the inheritance you carry. And then, once uncovered, you amend it—not primarily through words and mission statements, but through action. Through building. Through the choices you make and the value you create.

What you're building, in the end, is directional gravity. You cannot choose whether your children and grandchildren resist that gravity or compound it. That's their agency, and you must respect it. But you can establish enough pull that your family's trajectory becomes, across many different individual paths, the natural direction. Not train tracks that allow no deviation (or everyone on the same yacht), but a tilt in the field that makes certain futures feel more aligned than others.

The families that thrive across generations don't worship their history. They honor it while keeping their eyes forward. The past provides the anchoring context—the origin story that establishes identity and gives current choices authenticity. The future provides meaning—the horizon toward which all the building is aimed. The present is where the work gets done. This is why having an exciting future to build is so compelling for our children and grandchildren; a bigger future, as Dan Sullivan said, makes their present better.

What would it look like for your descendants—people you'll never meet—to know intuitively what it means to carry your family name? Not because you wrote it in a document, but because the stories were told, the values were embodied, and the behavior validated and compounded the narrative. Not because you controlled their choices, but because the gravity you established made certain directions feel more natural than others. This is true legacy—not what you leave, but *who* you leave and the direction they carry forward.

Principles

1. **Alignment requires a shared direction, not shared control or shared outcomes.** When families try to align through mandates and rigid expectations, they inevitably produce resistance. Control doesn't scale; it's limited by the bandwidth of those in charge. Influence, by contrast, can travel anywhere, across generations and geographies. A family aligned by direction can tolerate enormous diversity in how that direction gets expressed. Different vessels, different routes, same horizon. Direction enables growth; control prevents it.
2. **A family's culture, expressed through story and embodied through behavior, is the bridge between its ancestors' grit and its descendants' goals.** Capital transfers wealth. Culture transfers identity. When a family has a magnetic culture—built on stories of remote ancestors, lived values, and a clear sense of direction—people willingly identify with it. That attachment doesn't constrain them but to the contrary empowers and gives them an anchoring context for their choices and a direction for their building. Without culture, children will create their own identity, often in opposition to whatever exists. With it, they become the next chapter of an ongoing story.

Application Examples

These ideas matter most when translated from concept to concrete action. Below is a sampling of age-appropriate prompts to guide you with your children or grandchildren.

Get the full list at WealthTrapBook.com/list.

- **Ages 5–8**

  Tell bedtime stories about great-grandparents and great-great-grandparents. Focus on moments of courage, adventure, or difficulty overcome. Ask your child: "What do you think was the hardest part for them?" and "What do you think they would say if they could see you now?" Let these ancestors become familiar characters in your child's imagination—part of the cast of their mental world.

- **Ages 9–12**

  Create a family tree project together, but focus on stories rather than just names and dates. For each ancestor you can research, write down one thing they built, one challenge they overcame, or one way they helped others. Help your child see the pattern: "Notice how many of these people created something or helped someone through hard times. That's who we come from."

- **Ages 13–17**

  Have a conversation about the difference between a prescribed path and a shared direction. Ask: "What do you think our family actually stands for—not what we say, but what we do?" Listen without defending. Then ask: "What direction do you feel pulled toward? How might that connect to what our family has always been about?"

- **Ages 18–25**

  Invite them into the "excavation" work. Task them with researching one branch of the family tree and presenting their findings at a family gathering. Ask them to identify patterns: "What did the builders in our lineage have in common? What can we learn from those who struggled?" Let them contribute to the anchoring context rather than just passively receive it.

CHAPTER 7

Shared Language, Shared Meaning

Maurizio Gucci was forty-six years old when he walked up the marble steps to his Milan office on a March morning in 1995. He never made it inside. A gunman approached from behind, fired three shots into his back and a fourth into his head, then walked away. The hit had been ordered by his ex-wife. By then, the Gucci family had already lost control of the company that bore their name. What began as a Florentine leather workshop had become a global fashion empire—and then, over a few short decades, a bitter civil war. Uncles sued nephews. Sons informed on fathers for tax evasion. Siblings aligned with outside financiers against one another. Underneath the glamour, there was no shared sense of what Gucci was for beyond money and status. The business became a throne to seize, not a legacy to share. The assassination was just the loudest symptom of a family whose inner cohesion had already been murdered.[1]

The Shoen family's story is less cinematic, but just as gutting. Leonard Shoen founded U-Haul and raised twelve children across multiple marriages. From the outside, the business story looked like a classic American success: a simple idea—rentable moving trucks—turned into a household name. Inside the family, however, it devolved into decades of lawsuits, proxy battles, and estrangement. Children tried to oust their father. Siblings tried to wrest control from one another. There were boards, bylaws, and corporate counsel all along the way. What there *wasn't* was a shared understanding of what U-Haul meant or what it meant to be a Shoen. Governance became a weapon. The founder was eventually ousted from the very company his grit had built.[2]

Most families will (thankfully) never see anything so violent. Their version of the story will be far more likely to resemble the Strohs. Over five generations, the Stroh family built one of America's largest breweries, kick-started by Bernhard Stroh, an immigrant from Germany who arrived in Detroit in 1850 with $150. At its peak in the 1980s, the company was worth billions in today's dollars. The Stroh family had no headline scandal, no single villain, just a slow unraveling. Different branches of the family had different goals. Some wanted to expand aggressively, others to sell, others to hunker down and preserve. Advisors came and went. Deals were done. But there was no deep, shared language about why the business existed or what the family hoped it would be for beyond financial return. When the pressure mounted, there was nothing solid to lean on. Within a generation, Stroh Brewing was gone—sold off in pieces, the fortune that had taken 150 years to build largely evaporated. (The Stroh family lost over $700 million.[3])

You don't need murder to kill a legacy. You only need misalignment, compounded slowly, with enough money lying around to hide the damage until it can't be reversed. In each of these families, capital outlived culture. They had assets, structures, and experts. What was missing was a shared language for why the family had any of it in the first place.

Shared Wealth, Unshared Words

This is where most affluent families find themselves today—not in open civil war, but in a kind of polite fragmentation. The parents are asking one set of questions: *What should we do with our wealth? How do we protect what we built? What will our legacy be?* The rising generation is asking completely different questions: *What do I do with my life? How do I matter? How do I create something of my own?* Each side honestly believes they're talking about the same thing—responsibility, opportunity, purpose—but uses those words so differently that conversations become a series of near misses. Everyone leaves the room feeling that they have spoken and not been heard.

Shared wealth without shared language is like an armada with no agreed-upon heading. Each ship may be exquisitely designed, fully provisioned, and professionally crewed, but if everyone is steering toward a different horizon, the fleet eventually disappears into the fog—each vessel running its own private experiment until the fuel runs out.

Let's consider a specific example. By this point in the book, we've used the word "meaning" 137 times. (Yes, I counted.) We've talked about meaningful work, meaningful struggle, meaningful use of wealth, and more. Chances are, you nodded along because the term resonates. But if we paused and had you write down a one-sentence definition, your definition may not match ours. That's not really a problem in casual conversation. But it is a huge problem when you're trying to design a culture that will guide real decisions for your children, grandchildren, and beyond. The same thing happens inside families. For example, parents say "stewardship" and often mean "I feel a duty to manage these assets wisely so they don't harm you." Their children hear "stewardship" and translate it as "You expect me to babysit a pile of money I didn't ask for on terms I didn't choose." One word, two completely different experiences.

Before we can discuss shared language, we need to have a shared definition. For meaning, in the context of a multigenerational family, we're not referring to a mood or a slogan. It is not generic "happiness" or the warm tingle you might feel when being charitable. Meaning is *the experience of being responsibly necessary to a purpose that transcends the self and endures over time.* When your life feels meaningful, it is because you sense that:

1. something real and important is at stake;
2. your presence and effort genuinely matter to that thing; and
3. the thing itself will continue beyond you.

Each part of that definition matters. "Responsibly necessary" implies that you are not ornamental. If you vanished, someone would feel it. Your absence would have consequences; your contribution cannot be fully outsourced. "A purpose that transcends the self" means the aim is bigger than your personal comfort, ego, or preferences. Raising children, building an institution, advancing a field, serving a community—these are all purposes that reach beyond one person's interests and emotional state. And "endures over time" means the purpose is not over the moment you achieve a short-term goal. It has continuity. It stretches into a future where you might not be present, but your fingerprints could still be visible.

What Meaning Actually Requires

If that sounds abstract, we can make it structural (see figure 14). Meaning rests on three legs, like a stool. If any one of them is missing, the experience collapses. The first leg is agency: *I can choose and act.* The second leg is constraint: *My choices carry real cost.* The third leg is continuity: *The system I'm part of persists beyond me* (or as the saying goes, "to plant trees, under whose shade you do not expect to sit"). Put differently: I am free to move, my movement matters, and what I'm moving toward isn't going to disappear the moment I arrive. When all three are present, work, relationships, and sacrifices feel worthwhile. When one or more is missing, people (and especially teenagers and young adults) experience boredom, resentment, or drift—no matter how pleasant their circumstances appear.

THE THREE CONDITIONS OF MEANING

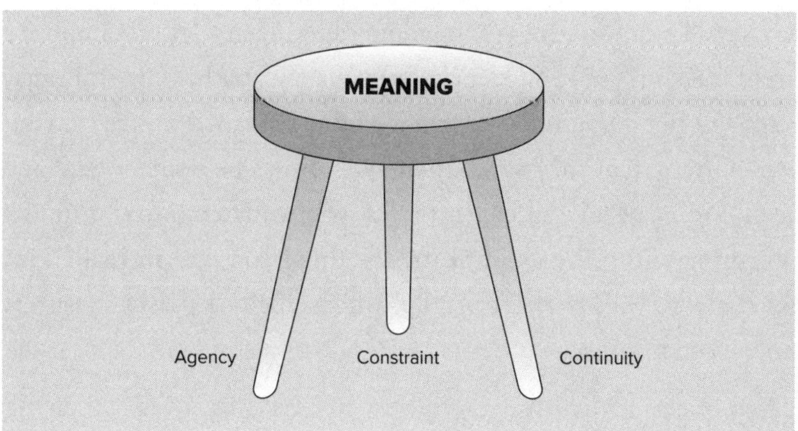

Figure 14

The agency leg is relatively straightforward. If you have no say, you cannot feel meaningfully involved. A child forced into the family business against their will might comply and might even perform well, but they will rarely describe their life as meaningful. The constraint leg is often misunderstood in affluent contexts. When money, staff, and opportunities are abundant, removing consequences becomes easy. People can make bad decisions and be quietly bailed out. Projects can fail and be papered over with capital. Children can dabble without ever having to see anything break. On the surface, this feels kind. Underneath, it corrodes meaning, because nothing really *costs* them anything. The continuity leg connects to Burke's idea of a partnership between the living, the dead, and the yet-to-be-born. If you're working inside a system that might be sold tomorrow or a family story that no one else seems to care about, it is hard to experience your own contribution as part of something enduring.

This is where shared language is most important. If parents and children do not use the same words to describe the fundamentals, they will engineer and experience very different environments. A parent may say, "I want to give you freedom" and mean, "I won't impose a career track on you; you can choose your own path." The child may hear, "I'm not going to be present or offer guidance; you're on your own." Or a parent may say, "There will always be a safety net," and mean, "You can take intelligent risks; you won't end up destitute if something fails." The child hears, "Nothing you do can really hurt you; someone will always clean it up," which quietly dissolves constraint and with it, meaning.

A Generational Contrast

You can see this clash vividly if you map what parents and next-gen heirs are actually asking themselves. Parents tend to frame their inner questions around wealth: *What do I do with what I've built? How do I protect it? How do I give back? How can I ensure my children are "taken care of"?* Their children, especially once they reach adulthood, frame their inner questions around life: *What do I do with my time and talent? How do I create something of my own? How do I make a difference?* When you put these two sets of questions side by side, they rarely overlap. One side hears, "You should be so grateful for the opportunities I've given you." The other hears, "Don't you trust that I'm capable of creating my own opportunities?" One side offers a safety net. The other side experiences it as a ceiling.

GENERATIONAL CONTRAST CIRCLES

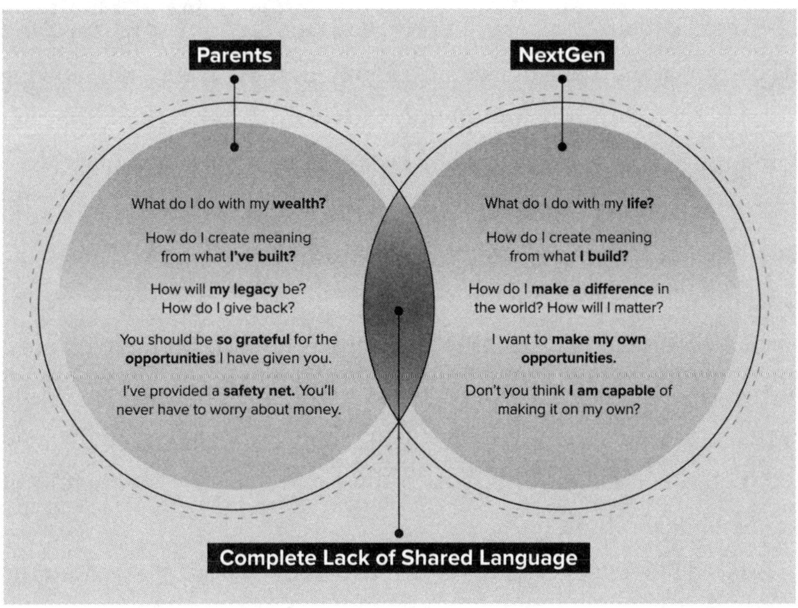

Figure 15

This is the mismatch captured in the Generational Contrast Circles (see figure 15). If you listen closely at a family meeting where finances, governance, or futures are being discussed, you can often hear the circles talking past each other. Parents say things like, "We need to make sure this doesn't get squandered," "You kids have no idea what it took to get here," or "The tax man is waiting if we screw this up." Children say things like, "I don't want to be trapped by this," "I want to do something that's mine," or "I don't see myself in any of this." Both sets of concerns are legitimate. Both are incomplete on their own. We risk talking past one another unless we develop a shared language.

The temptation for the older generation is to answer purpose questions with preservation language and to respond to heart-level questions with balance sheet answers. A son says, "I want my work to matter," and Dad replies, "You really need to sit in on more of the quarterly meetings." A daughter says, "I don't want this money to own me," and the conversation veers into lectures about diversification, "not blowing it," and how much is being spent on advisors. Parents think they are doing the prudent thing—they're trying to keep everyone safe. Their children often hear something very different: that they're more anxious about preserving past success than about exploring and investing in who their children are becoming. Younger generations are just as prone to distortion in the other direction. They see all the structures, all the caution, and assume it's just about hoarding, without taking the time to understand the near-bankruptcies, sleepless nights, and very real fears that sit underneath their parents' obsession with not losing what was built.

Shared language enables the two circles to overlap. It provides the family with a way to discuss preservation in terms of purpose and purpose in terms of preservation. "We don't want you to waste what we built" can become, "We want you to use this wealth to build things that matter, not to numb yourself." "I don't want to be controlled by this" can become, "I want to do something new; help me see how it fits here." The underlying concerns don't go away. They finally have words that the other side can hear.

One simple exercise is to literally draw the two circles. Have the senior generation write down the five or six questions that keep them up at night about the family and its wealth. Have the rising generation do the same. Then put those questions on the wall and ask together: Where do these intersect? Where might an honest answer to your question also help answer mine? You'll often find that both sides care deeply about things like contribution, character, and cohesion—they've just never said it in the same way. The work of shared language is to surface that latent overlap and name it.

From Talking Past to Talking With

The tragedy of the Guccis, the Shoens, and the Strohs was not that they lacked intelligence, resources, or even good intentions. It was (among other things) that they had no shared vocabulary for the questions that mattered most. When pressure came—and pressure always comes—there was nothing beneath the legal structures and financial capital to hold them together. Our version of the same failure is everywhere. Parents and children sitting in the same room, using terms like "responsibility," "opportunity," "legacy," and "freedom," and meaning different things by each one. The conversations feel productive in the moment. Everyone nods. Everyone leaves. And nothing actually aligns, because no one paused long enough to ask: *What do we actually mean when we say that?*

Shared language is not about scripting your family's conversations or creating a glossary that everyone must memorize. It's about doing the slower, harder work of surfacing assumptions. When you say "legacy," what do you picture? When your daughter hears it, what does she feel? When you talk about "making a difference," are you imagining the same thing your son imagines? These gaps are evidence of being human. The failure is never bothering to notice and narrow them.

This chapter's frameworks give you a way to diagnose where communication is breaking down. If your child seems disengaged despite having every opportunity, ask yourself: Which leg of the stool is missing? Do they have genuine agency, or are they following a script you wrote? Do their choices carry real consequences, or does the family wealth absorb every cost? Do they see themselves as part of something that will endure, or does the whole enterprise feel like it could evaporate the moment you're gone?

If conversations with your adult children feel like two ships passing in the night, create some contrast circles. Write down your questions. Have them write down theirs. Put them on the table and look for the overlap that's been hiding beneath the surface. You may discover that you're both deeply concerned about things like contribution, character, or purpose—you've just never found the words to say it in a way the other side could hear.

This is the work that structures cannot do for you. You can hire the best attorneys, build the most sophisticated trusts, and retain a fleet of advisors. None of it will create shared meaning. Shared meaning is built-in conversation, reinforced through story, and sustained by the slow accumulation of moments in which someone feels genuinely heard. It cannot be outsourced. It cannot be scheduled into a single annual meeting. It has to become part of how your family talks—not just about money, but about life.

Perfect agreement is not the goal. Families are not meant to be ideological monoliths where everyone believes the same things and wants the same outcomes. (Remember: armada, not yacht.) The goal is mutual intelligibility: the ability to understand what someone else means even when you disagree, and to be understood in return. When that foundation exists, conflict becomes productive rather than corrosive. Disagreements can be navigated because everyone is at least working from the same map, even if they're advocating for different destinations.

Without shared language, influence is impossible. All that remains is control, and control doesn't scale. It's constrained by the bandwidth of those in charge and the boundaries of existing governance structures. You cannot control your family from the grave. But your influence can compound long after you're gone, carried forward in the stories that get retold, the definitions that get internalized, and the questions that your descendants learn to ask themselves. That influence begins with language, with taking the time, now, to say what you actually mean—and to listen long enough to learn what your children actually hear.

The Strohs had 150 years of brewing expertise. The Shoens had a business model that dominated its industry. The Guccis had one of the most recognizable brands in the world. None of it was enough to hold the family together when the language failed. Your family's most valuable asset can't be found on a balance sheet. It's found in the shared understanding that allows you to row in the same direction when the water gets rough. Build that, and the rest becomes possible. Neglect it, and no amount of capital can save you from slow dissolution.

Principles

1. **Families fall apart when they lose a common vocabulary.** When family members use the same words to mean different things, conversations become a series of near misses. Parents talk about "responsibility" and mean protecting assets; children hear the word and feel the weight of expectations they never chose. Over time, these small misalignments compound into major rifts. Shared vocabulary doesn't guarantee agreement, but it makes genuine understanding possible—and understanding is the foundation on which everything else is built.
2. **Meaning must be communicated through story, not dictated through rules.** You cannot hand your children a laminated card

with the family values and expect those values to shape their lives. Values stated as abstractions—hard work, integrity, service, and so on—are easy to nod at and even easier to ignore. Values embedded in stories, by contrast, become part of how people see the world. When your children know the story of the ancestor who sacrificed, the founder who persevered, the relative who chose principle over convenience, those narratives become reference points for their own decisions. Rules tell people what to do. Stories show them who to be. And identity, once formed, guides behavior far more reliably than any compliance mechanism ever could.

Application Examples

These ideas matter most when translated from concept to concrete action. Below is a sampling of age-appropriate prompts to guide you with your children or grandchildren.

Get the full list at WealthTrapBook.com/list.

- **Ages 5–8**

  Pick a word your family uses often—like *work* or *help*—and ask your child what they think it means. Listen without correcting. Then share what it means to you, using a simple story. Let them see that words carry stories inside them.

- **Ages 9–12**

  Play a definition game at dinner. Choose a word that matters to your family—like *generosity* or *courage*—and have everyone write down their own one-sentence definition without showing anyone else. Then read them aloud. Notice where the definitions overlap and where they differ. Use the differences as a starting point for conversation, not correction.

- **Ages 13–17**

  Have a direct conversation about the three conditions for meaning. Explain the framework, then ask: "Where in your life right now do you feel all three of these? Where do you feel like one is missing?" Listen more than you talk. The goal is to understand their experience, not to fix it in the moment.

- **Ages 18–25**

  Sit down together and draw the contrast circles. You write down the three to five questions that keep you up at night about the family and its future. Have them write down the three to five questions that keep them up at night about their own life and direction. Place both lists on the table and identify any overlap. Where might an honest answer to your question also help answer theirs? Use this as the beginning of a longer conversation about what you're each actually trying to figure out—and where you might be able to help each other.

CHAPTER 8

A Family Operating System

Chris Smith grew up in a small Arizona town where everyone knew everyone—and everyone had a story about what it meant to be a Smith. His family carried both strength and struggle. Some of his siblings battled addiction and found themselves in difficult circumstances that, in a tight-knit community, quickly became part of the narrative attached to their last name. By the time Chris was a teenager, assumptions often came before introductions. "Oh, you're a Smith?" people would say—filling in the rest before they even knew him.[1] He felt the weight of expectations that weren't his, shaped by patterns that had been forming long before he arrived.

Chris experienced deep loss, including the heartbreaking deaths of two of his brothers due to addiction. He saw firsthand how unaddressed pain can ripple through generations when there aren't tools to interrupt it. And somewhere in the middle of that grief, he made a quiet decision: The story didn't have to end the way it had always gone. In his early twenties, a mentor told him that in every family, someone eventually chooses to change the narrative. In that moment, Chris felt a conviction rise in him—that he would be the one to redefine what it meant to be a Smith.

Melissa, Chris's wife, grew up in a very different environment—the oldest of nine children in a devout, hardworking household. Her home was steady and full of responsibility, and, like many families doing their best, it had unspoken patterns woven into daily life. Difficult topics weren't always talked about openly. Everyone stayed busy, focused on what needed to be done, and carried on with good intentions. As the oldest, Melissa learned early to be capable and composed. Somewhere along the way, though, she quietly absorbed a message her parents never intended: that keeping things together mattered, and that bringing up hard questions might create unwanted discomfort.

When Chris and Melissa married young—she was twenty, he was twenty-two—they shared an early vision of building something intentional together. They wanted a family defined not by inherited dysfunction or unspoken expectations, but by purpose. Within a few years, though, reality set in. Two babies arrived in rapid succession. Life became a blur of survival. And then, just weeks after their second son was born, Chris told Melissa he wasn't sure he wanted to be married anymore.

They separated. For months, divorce seemed inevitable. But a marriage counselor said something that neither of them had heard from anyone else: "You have something worth fighting for." That simple sentence cracked open a door. They rebuilt their marriage slowly, painfully, intentionally. And in the process, they began to consider a question that would eventually reshape their entire family: *How do we stop drifting and start designing?*

The answer, they discovered, was that love alone wasn't enough. Good intentions weren't enough. Even a clear vision of who they wanted to become wasn't enough.

They needed a system.

Why Systems Matter

Perhaps the most memorable line in James Clear's book, *Atomic Habits*, is this: "You do not rise to the level of your goals. You fall to the level of your systems." The observation applies to fitness, productivity, and business. It applies with equal force to families.

Most parents seemingly assume that values are transmitted through proximity. If we love our kids, spend time with them, model good behavior, and occasionally share our beliefs, surely they'll absorb what matters. This assumption feels reasonable. It's also, in most cases, wrong—or at least incomplete. Values do not transmit reliably through osmosis. They transmit through systems: repeated behaviors, structured conversations, rituals that encode meaning into the rhythm of daily life. Without those systems, even the best intentions dissipate into the chaos of ordinary existence.

Consider what happens in a business without a well-defined operating system. Employees show up, but they don't know why the organization exists or where their energies are best spent. Leaders have a vision, but it never reaches the front lines. Meetings meander. Priorities shift weekly. Energy scatters in a dozen directions. The business might survive for a while on the founder's force of will, but it cannot scale, and it certainly cannot outlast the founder. This is why serious companies invest in crafting clear operating systems—structured frameworks for alignment, communication, and accountability.

Families face the same challenge, but most never think of it in these terms. We would never expect a medium- or large-sized company to function without clear systems for decision-making and communication. Yet we routinely see families—complex human systems with their own histories, conflicts, and competing priorities—trying to function on nothing more than love and good intentions. When things start to drift, we may blame the kids, the culture, or the busyness of modern life. We rarely blame the absence of a system, because we never knew we needed one.

Back to business for a moment. The reality is that every enterprise has an operating system, even if it's undefined. There are unspoken rules and unplanned processes. Particularly for smaller companies, dysfunction from lack of clarity is just assumed to be part of the expected chaos of an adventurous start-up. That's certainly how I experienced the early years of Libertas Network, the nonprofit I founded in 2011. But moving from the start-up phase to become an organization with over two hundred people operating several business units—each with different programs serving families and teaching kids the principles of human flourishing—created growing pains I could not ignore. I realized, a little too late, that we needed a better system.

Libertas Network's growth created complexity that outpaced our informal ways of staying aligned. We found ourselves in too many meetings without clear agendas and action items, with too many priorities competing for attention, and too little definition about who owned what decisions. We ended up incorporating the Entrepreneur Operating System (EOS) to establish a standardized structure: a meeting rhythm, a shared vocabulary, and a way to surface and resolve issues before they festered. It let us sing from the same sheet of music.

The same principle applies at home. A family that wants to align effort between two generations and transmit purpose across several more yet unborn needs more than a mission statement on the wall. It needs an operating system that turns that mission into daily, weekly, and annual reinforcement rhythms.

Back to the Farm

To grasp why this matters so much now, it helps to recall what families once had that most families today have lost.

For most of human history, where nearly 90 percent of people worked in agriculture, necessity *was* the operating system. The farm demanded attention. Animals needed feeding before dawn. Crops required tending. Weather imposed constraints. Consequences were immediate and unmistakable: If you didn't work, the family didn't eat. Children didn't need to be taught the value of hard work through lectures or incentive programs. They learned it by watching their parents, then by doing it themselves, because survival required it. The system was invisible precisely because it was all-encompassing. Few ever sat down to discuss "family values" around the dinner table—the values were embedded in the work itself, reinforced every single day by the demands of the environment.

Necessity, therefore, is the original operating system. In such an environment, the system provides feedback to the individual. Slack off, and you'd see the result in the harvest. Make a foolish decision, and the family would pay for it. Contribute meaningfully, and the evidence was right there in front of you—in the full barn, the healthy livestock, the food on the table. Children developed competence because competence was required. They developed a sense of responsibility because irresponsibility exacted immediate costs. The environment itself was the teacher.

Wealth changes the physics entirely. When money removes necessity, it also removes the invisible operating system that necessity provided. The arrows reverse (see figure 16). Instead of the environment pressing inward on the family, demanding response and adaptation, the family now must press outward on the environment, reshaping it to suit their preferences. Problems that once required effort and ingenuity can be solved with a phone call. Discomfort that once built character can be avoided entirely. Children grow up in a world where the natural feedback loops have been severed. They can coast indefinitely without ever confronting the consequences of their choices, because the family's resources absorb every impact.

NECESSITY VS. ABUNDANCE

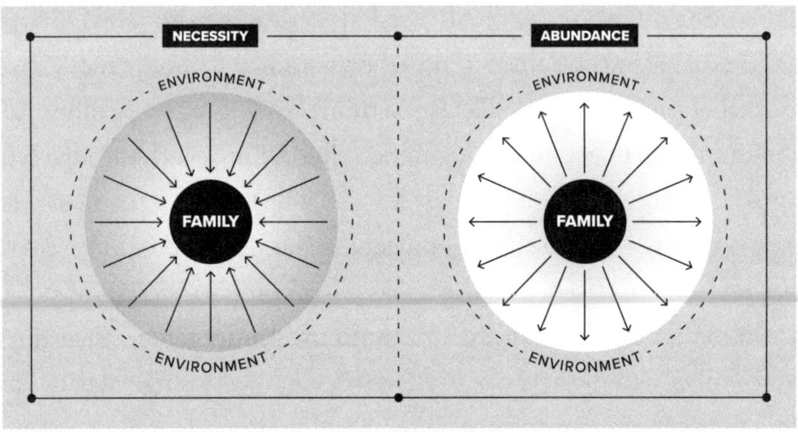

Figure 16

To be clear, prosperity is a genuine good—it creates options, funds education, enables generosity, provides security, and results in myriad more benefits. But prosperity without a replacement operating system produces drift. The values that were once embedded in daily necessity now float free, untethered to any structure that reinforces them. First, the values are embodied in the generation that built the wealth (people who, whether they knew it or not, had an operating system to support that wealth creation). Then those values are remembered by the children who watched their parents sacrifice. Then they are interpreted—loosely, selectively—by the grandchildren who heard the stories. Then they become optional, one lifestyle choice among many, for the great-grandchildren who inherit the resources but not the system that gave the resources meaning. Without a system, you don't lose your values to opposition—you lose them to irrelevance.

This is the drift problem that haunts affluent families. Not a sudden collapse, but a slow fade. No one revolts. The wealth doesn't disappear overnight. The family just gradually loses the invisible architecture that once held everything together. By the time the drift becomes visible—in entitlement, in conflict, in the quiet despair of heirs who have everything except purpose—the system can feel too late to reverse.

The Cost of No System

Without an operating system, families experience a predictable pattern of decay. The specifics vary, but the trajectory is consistent.

The drift comes first. Communication becomes shallow. Conversations stay on the surface—schedules, logistics, the occasional polite inquiry about school or work. Deeper questions go unasked because there's no structure that invites them. Family members begin to assume they know what others are thinking, but those assumptions are often wrong. The shared understanding that once felt effortless starts to fray. The shared language we covered in the previous chapter is nonexistent.

Then comes incentive inversion. When financial distributions aren't tied to development or contribution, capital becomes unconditional approval. The message, however unintended, is that the family will support you regardless of what you do with your life. What gets reinforced is consumption, not creation. Children learn to extract resources from the system rather than build their own capacity. No one likely sets out to become an extractor—but incentives shape behavior, and unexamined ones shape it invisibly.

Governance vacuums follow. When decision rights aren't explicit, power flows to whoever is loudest, wealthiest, or most willing to apply emotional pressure. Families that pride themselves on avoiding "corporate" governance structures often end up with something worse: informal hierarchies where influence operates through guilt, triangulation, or passive aggression. Control gets mistaken for leadership. Compliance gets mistaken for unity.

And so, identity begins to collapse. When a person's primary relationship to their family is receiving—when they are not needed, not contributing, not building—their sense of self starts to erode. Even capable, well-intentioned young adults can rot internally if they have no role to fill. The family's resources become a ceiling rather than a floor: Instead of providing a foundation from which to build, they provide a cocoon from which there is no reason to emerge.

Taylor has seen this pattern in his own extended family—175 people connected to a family office that became, over time, purely a financial operation. His father thankfully breathed life back into the system by becoming a successful value creator himself—someone others could look up to and emulate. But even that wasn't enough to reverse the broader drift. The family office president, once a mentor who met weekly with a few younger family members to offer guidance and encouragement, became so overwhelmed by administrative complexity—tax deadlines, estate planning, the exponential growth of legal structures as each generation expanded—that no bandwidth was left for human capital. The mentorship stopped. The younger generation was left to drift.

This is what happens when families have financial systems but no human capital operating system. The money gets managed. The people do not.

Building the Replacement

If necessity was the original operating system, and wealth has dissolved it, then families must intentionally build what the farm once provided naturally. This is not optional. It is not a nice-to-have for families who are particularly organized or relationally inclined.

Necessity is a structural requirement for any family that wants to transmit purpose across generations, the process by which builders are formed.

The good news is that building a family operating system is not as complicated as it might sound. No elaborate governance documents or flowcharts are required to get started. At its foundation, three things are required: a commitment to regular communication, a set of repeatable rituals, and the discipline to sustain them over time. For affluent families, the system will eventually need to incorporate greater sophistication around governance, capital deployment, and distribution incentives. But even the most complex multigenerational operating system is built on the same bedrock: people talking to each other consistently, with intention, about what matters. Start there. The sophistication your family's resources demand can be layered onto a foundation of consistent, intentional connection—but without that foundation, no amount of structural complexity will hold.

Chris and Melissa discovered this through trial and error. After rebuilding their marriage, they began asking what it would take to raise children who understood what it meant to be a Smith—not the old narrative of chaos and addiction, but a new narrative of intention and creation. Chris had been coaching businesses on brand identity, helping companies articulate who they were and what they stood for. One day, a client told him that the work they'd done together would shape the company for the next hundred years. On the drive home, Chris wondered: *Could the same frameworks that clarify a business's identity work for a family?*

He took his family through his own process. They went to an offsite at his office, gathered around a whiteboard, and asked themselves the fundamental questions: Who are we? What do we stand for? What do we want to be known for? By the end of that session, they had something they'd never had before—a shared vocabulary, a declared identity, a sense of direction they had chosen rather than inherited. They called it their "family brand."

But Melissa will tell you that the brand itself wasn't the breakthrough. The breakthrough was what came after: the system that turned those words into daily life. Without the system, the brand would have become just another document filed away and forgotten. With the system, it became the household's operating rhythm. Their system is built on cadences: daily, weekly, monthly, and annually. Every morning at breakfast, the family recites their values together. It takes less than a minute. The words become familiar, then internalized, then automatic. This is how shared language forms—through repetition that embeds meaning into muscle memory.

Weekly, Chris and Melissa hold two kinds of check-ins. The first is a family meeting: brief, structured, focused on gratitude, acknowledgment of one another, upcoming logistics, and any challenges someone wants help solving. The second is individual: Each parent meets one-on-one with each child to ask two questions borrowed from a business book on team leadership. "What's important to you this week? How can I support you?" That's it. No lectures, no performance reviews, no interrogation about grades. Just presence, attention, and an open door.

Melissa recalls her youngest daughter participating in these check-ins when she was barely three years old. The child couldn't articulate career goals or life priorities, but she could say what mattered to her that week and how her parents could help. (In one case, it was as simple as her wanting some chocolate from Dad's stash, and Mom could help by lifting her up to get a piece.) The point was never sophistication. The point was building the muscle of communication, one week at a time, until it became the normal way the family operated.

Monthly, they do kid dates: one-on-one time with each child, kept deliberately simple so it actually happens. A bike ride. A trip to feed the ducks. Nothing elaborate, nothing that requires extensive planning. Just consistent presence. Annually, they gather for a more intensive ritual around the new year that includes vision boards, words and quotes for the year, and goals that the weekly check-ins will then reinforce. The annual session sets direction; the weekly rhythms sustain it.

This is what a family operating system looks like at its simplest—and for many families, it may be enough. Not a binder full of policies, but a set of habits that create space for the conversations that matter. The policies create structure and rhythm instead of control and bureaucracy. But for families with significant wealth, the operating system must also contend with the perverse incentives that abundance introduces. When resources remove natural consequences, the system needs mechanisms that tie capital access to development, create real stakes where the environment no longer provides them, and ensure the family's resources function as a launchpad rather than a cushion. The rituals of connection remain the foundation—but they must be paired with the governance and incentive structures that keep abundance from unraveling what you've built.

The Engine of Human Progress

There is a deeper reason why this matters—one that extends beyond any individual family's well-being.

Healthy families have always been the engine of human progress. The great advances in science, commerce, art, and social organization have overwhelmingly emerged from cultures where families functioned as crucibles of capability and character. The Medici family funded the Renaissance, but more importantly, they raised generation after generation of children who understood that wealth existed to build lasting institutions. The Rockefellers produced three generations of consequential builders before the drift set in. The Bach family produced not only Johann Sebastian but over fifty professional musicians across seven generations. It would be foolish to write this off as genetics or happenstance. Families that invest in their children's development, that transmit values and knowledge across generations, that deploy their resources toward building rather than merely consuming—these families produce the builders who carry civilization forward.

Embedded in their culture and operating systems was a core directionality of purpose—a shared orientation that shaped how each generation understood its role and responsibilities. That directionality didn't remain abstract but became embodied in the attitudes and behavior of individual family members, internalized through the rituals and rhythms of daily life until it operated from the inside out. Once embodied, directionality becomes decentralized. No longer dependent on a patriarch's force of will or a family council's expectation, orientation empowers individuals to exercise full autonomy in determining how and where they create value in the world, while remaining anchored to something larger than themselves. The family, and its operating system, become an innovation sandbox—an environment where human capital is developed and then unleashed to experiment, take risks, and pursue individual self-actualization. Individual pursuits may be remarkably diverse—one sibling builds companies, another practices medicine, a third creates art—yet an emergent order holds. That order is sustained by each person's belonging to and felt responsibility for a shared direction. This shared directionality and the operating system that embodies it serve a dual function that first enables individuals to make sense of their own lives within a larger context—to understand why their work matters beyond personal achievement. The shared directionality also enables them to make sense of generational resources and capabilities, seeing inherited wealth not as an entitlement to be consumed but as capital to be productively deployed. In this regard, a family's human capital operating system becomes the backbone for managing all other forms of capital. Without it, financial and philanthropic resources lack coherent direction. With it, every form of capital the family possesses finds its purpose.

ENGINE OF HUMAN PROGRESS

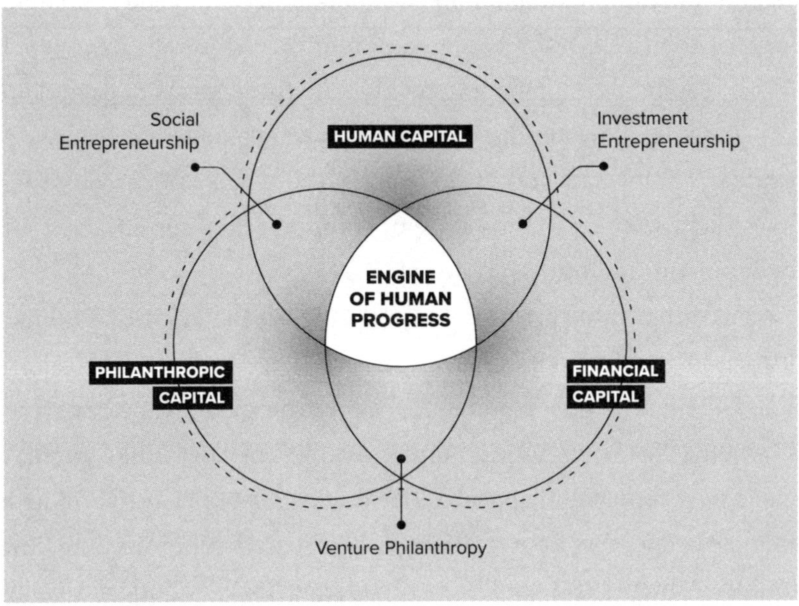

Figure 17

We can visualize this as the intersection of three forms of capital (see figure 17). Human capital is the capability, character, and purpose developed in family members—the skills they build, the values they embody, and the meaning they pursue. Investment capital is the financial resources the family deploys toward ventures that create economic value and generate returns. Philanthropic capital is the resources and energy directed toward serving others, such as charitable giving and community involvement.

At the intersection of these three lies the engine of human progress. When a family develops a strong directionality of purpose, embedded in an operating system, its human capital becomes empowered to leverage investment capital and philanthropic capital more effectively. When investment capital generates returns, it funds both further human capital development and expanded philanthropic reach. Philanthropic engagement that connects family members to needs beyond themselves deepens their sense of meaning and reinforces the values on which human capital development depends. The three forms of capital are typically treated by families as separate buckets to be managed independently. But when working in concert, they become interconnected flows that create a virtuous cycle of compounding impact and open up opportunities for derivative value creation.

Derivative value creation is what enables the engine of human progress to truly compound. When the three forms of capital are siloed, there is no opportunity to identify synergies or capture derivative value. But when unified under a coherent operating system, a whole new dimension appears. The first order of derivative value is financial—income, appreciation, risk-adjusted compounding, and liquidity—but its real output is a broader optionality budget: surplus resources that can be redeployed into ventures and commitments that would otherwise be out of reach. The second order is capability—skills, judgment, agency, discipline, networks, and a reputation for competence—which increases each individual's value-creation capacity. The third order is system: a multigenerational operating capacity that builds culture, shared language, trust, governance, conflict resilience, and alignment, strengthening a family's ability to coordinate and compound across generations. This is the rarest and most valuable form, because it outlasts any individual contributor. When these three orders reinforce one another under a shared directionality, a crucial insight emerges: Capability and multigenerational operating capacity are not downstream benefits of financial returns but upstream multipliers. Money compounds. Capability and culture compound the compounding.

This is why an operating system matters so much. Without the structures that develop human capital—the communication rhythms, the designed struggles, the rituals of meaning—families default to managing the three forms of capital in siloed isolation. The investment side might perform adequately, at least for a while. The philanthropic side might generate positive feelings and public reaction. But without strong human capital integrated with the other forms of capital, the whole system eventually runs down. The investment decisions become more about preservation than creation. The philanthropy becomes more about status and access than about genuine problem-solving. And the family itself drifts toward the decay we described earlier.

An operating system is what keeps human capital at the center. It's what ensures that conversations happen, that values are transmitted, and that each generation is challenged to become builders rather than beneficiaries. The operating system transforms the family from a passive recipient of inherited wealth into an active engine of progress—not only for themselves, but for everyone their building eventually touches.

Start Small, but Start

If you feel overwhelmed by the idea of implementing a family operating system, you're not alone. Most parents are already stretched thin. The idea of adding another set of meetings and rituals to an already chaotic schedule, or rearchitecting governance structures and inheritance decisions, can feel like one more burden in an impossible load. But here's what Melissa learned from the families she and Chris began coaching (see FamilyBrand.com): The families that succeeded weren't the ones who implemented elaborate systems overnight. They were the ones who started small and stayed consistent.

If weekly one-on-one check-ins feel like too much, start with just the two questions at dinner once a week: "What's important to you right now?

How can I support you?" If a formal family meeting sounds exhausting, just add a few minutes to something you already do together—a car ride to church or a walk after dinner—and use that time to ask about challenges and wins. If reciting family values every morning feels forced, pick one phrase that captures who you want to be and repeat it together on the way to school. The specific format matters far less than the consistency.

James Clear's concept of habit stacking applies here. Don't try to build a new structure from scratch; attach new practices to existing routines. If you already eat breakfast together, add the values recitation. If you already drive to activities together, make that the time for a one-on-one conversation. If you already gather for holidays, append the annual vision-setting to that tradition.

Families are enterprises, but they need not be run like a corporation. The goal, rather, is to be intentional about the things that won't happen unless you're intentional about them. Living on a farm forced those conversations and taught those lessons automatically. Having wealth does not. You have to build the replacement yourself.

Chris set out to change the narrative of what it meant to be a Smith. He didn't do it through willpower alone. He did it, alongside Melissa, by building a system to embed the new narrative into his family's daily life—one breakfast, one check-in, one kid date at a time. The story of his upbringing wasn't erased, nor should it be; it's part of his story, and that of his children. But it was replaced—with intention, with structure, with a rhythm that made the new chapter far more real and rewarding.

You can do the same by building whatever system fits your family's rhythms, your children's ages, and your available bandwidth. The specific practices matter less than the underlying commitment: to communicate regularly, to reinforce what matters, and to create the structures that necessity once provided and wealth has dissolved. On the farm, feedback was built into the environment—you knew immediately whether your efforts were sufficient because the crops grew or they didn't, and the animals thrived or they didn't. Abundance silences such feedback. When the external world no longer imposes consequences, families must generate their own internal signals: the check-ins, the rituals, the conversations that surface what would otherwise remain hidden. Without that intentional structure, children default to the path of least resistance—and in a world of abundance, that path leads nowhere.

Your children are watching. They are absorbing, right now, a sense of what your family is about. The question is whether that sense is being shaped by intention or by accident. An operating system is how you choose intention.

Principles

1. **Systems preserve culture better than sentiment.** Love is necessary but not sufficient. Good intentions do not reliably transmit across generations. What is transmitted is what gets repeated: conversations that happen weekly, values recited often, and rituals performed regularly. Systems encode meaning into the rhythm of ordinary life, where it can be absorbed and internalized rather than merely heard and forgotten. The families that sustain purpose across generations are not the ones who feel the most strongly about their values; they are the ones who build structures that reinforce those values when no one is paying attention.
2. **Alignment is sustained through rituals, roles, and relationships that reinforce shared purpose.** A family operating system is a set of repeatable practices that creates the conditions for alignment: regular communication that surfaces what's really going on, defined moments for goal setting and reflection, and one-on-one connection that makes each person feel known and supported. These rituals create the foundation from which

freedom can be meaningfully exercised. A family without these structures is like an armada without a heading—each ship technically free, but collectively adrift.

Application Examples

These ideas matter most when translated from concept to concrete action. Below is a sampling of age-appropriate prompts to guide you with your children or grandchildren.

Get the full list at WealthTrapBook.com/list.

- **Ages 5–8**
  Start a simple daily ritual: one sentence that captures what your family stands for, repeated together at breakfast or bedtime. Keep it short enough for young children to memorize. Your family values might also have actions assigned to them to make it fun for kids; if "the Boyack family is strong," then we all might flex our arms together, for example.
- **Ages 9–12**
  Introduce a weekly check-in with two questions: "What's important to you this week? How can I help?" Keep it casual, such as during a car ride or over a snack. The goal is to build the habit of reflective conversation, not to conduct a formal interview. Follow through on whatever support you offer; consistency builds trust.
- **Ages 13–17**
  Involve them in designing the family's operating rhythms. Ask something like: "What would help you feel more connected to what our family is about? What kind of regular conversation would actually be useful to you?" Teenagers are more likely to engage with systems they helped create than systems imposed on them. Be willing to adapt based on their input.

- **Ages 18–25**

  As they launch into adulthood, shift from parent-led check-ins to mutual accountability. Share what you're working on and struggling with; invite them to do the same. The relationship becomes more peer-like, but the rhythm of regular connection can continue. Ask them what structures are helping them stay aligned with their own goals, and share what's working for you. Model lifelong learning about how to live intentionally.

CHAPTER 9

Joyful Struggle

In the early 1990s, scientists sealed themselves inside Biosphere 2, a massive glass enclosure in the Arizona desert designed to simulate earth's ecosystems. The experiment was meant to test whether humans could survive in a self-contained environment—a dress rehearsal for potential space colonization. Inside the structure, researchers created rainforests, savannas, and oceans. They controlled temperature, humidity, and atmospheric composition. Everything was optimized.

And then the trees started falling over.

The trees in Biosphere 2 grew quickly in the controlled environment. They shot up toward the glass ceiling, their leaves lush and green. But before reaching maturity, many of them simply collapsed. They couldn't support their own weight. When researchers examined the fallen trees, they discovered something fascinating: The trees had failed to develop what botanists call "stress wood"—the dense, reinforced cellular structure that forms when trees are buffeted by wind. In nature, as a tree bends and flexes against gusts and storms, it responds by producing higher concentrations of cellulose, building strength exactly where it's needed. The stress literally makes the tree stronger.

Inside the sealed biosphere, there was no wind. The air was still. The trees had all the resources they needed to grow—water, nutrients, and light—but they lacked the one thing that would make them resilient. Without stress, they grew fast but fragile. They looked healthy right up until the moment they crumbled.

The parallel to raising children in abundance is almost too obvious to state, but obvious truths are often the ones we most need to hear. When we remove friction from our children's lives—when we optimize their environment so much that they never have to struggle—we may be producing the human equivalent of Biosphere 2 trees: impressive growth with no structural integrity. They look fine until life's inevitable winds arrive. And then they fall.

The System That Shaped a Builder

Preston Troutt grew up in Dallas, the oldest of three children. His father had built a successful telecom company from nothing. The family had resources. They could have made Preston's childhood very comfortable.

Instead, his father created a basketball team.

When Preston and his younger brother showed aptitude for the sport around third and fourth grade, their dad didn't just sign them up for the local rec league. He brought in a former coach to evaluate whether the boys could compete at the highest level. When the assessment came back positive, he founded the Texas Titans, a travel basketball program that would consume most of Preston's childhood and adolescence.

The Titans weren't a casual endeavor. During summers, Preston arrived at training at eight a.m. and left at three p.m., four days a week. The schedule rotated between three-hour practices, ninety minutes of strength and conditioning, and ninety minutes of skills work. The team traveled constantly, competing against the best youth players in the country.

The program demanded more than physical excellence. Speakers came in weekly to address the players on topics ranging from media training to professional etiquette. Someone taught them how interviews work, how to handle questions at halftime when emotions run high, and how to present themselves. These were elementary and middle school students being trained like professionals.

Preston's father never sat him down and explained the philosophy behind all of this. He didn't hear lectures about building character or developing resilience. The system simply existed, and Preston operated within it. Looking back, he recognizes what was happening: His father had engineered an environment where struggle was constant, feedback was immediate, and pursuing excellence was the only option.

"I think so much of what my dad saw," Preston reflected, "was what it could do for us. We were with so many different types of people, all on the same team, all working toward a shared goal of not just being a good team, but being the best team in the country."[1] But the struggle was real. Preston wanted to quit at least once—around seventh grade, when the relentlessness of it all became overwhelming. His coaches and his father talked him through it. They painted a picture of what perseverance could produce: a college basketball career, yes, but more importantly, a certain kind of person. He caught the vision (at least as much as a seventh grader could) and stayed.

Then came the injuries. During Preston's sophomore year, right before a major tournament, he nearly broke his ankle. His junior year, early in the season, he tore his shoulder and had to play through it with tape for the rest of the year. His brother's injury history was even worse—five consecutive years of surgeries from seventh grade through junior year. Both brothers made it to college basketball, but neither had the careers they'd envisioned. Preston tore both of his hips during his freshman and sophomore year at Penn and barely played. He didn't score a single point. His brother tore his hip again freshman year and had to quit when doctors began talking about a hip replacement—something that actually came to pass a few years later. They had stuck it out to the very end, only stopping when their bodies forced them to.

By conventional metrics, the basketball experiment failed. Preston didn't become a professional athlete. The thousands of hours, the grueling summers, the injuries—none of it produced the outcome that might have seemed, to an outsider, like the point. But Preston doesn't see it that way. "While we didn't really go play the career that we wanted," he said, "I think we're both so thankful that there's so much that we can point back to. Thank the Lord we stuck with that. Because it really did just build so much character. It built this layer of what hard work is and what it looks like."

The Titans weren't really about basketball. They were about building the kind of person who could face anything—who had been tested, who had struggled alongside others toward a shared goal, and who had learned that excellence requires sacrifice. The operating system Preston's father created was one for character formation, and it worked precisely because the struggle was real.

Why Struggle Feels Like Love

Here is a truth that cuts against every protective instinct parents possess: When you shield your children from difficulty, you are not loving them. You are weakening them.

This is hard to accept. When your child is struggling—with a difficult class, a demanding coach, or a project that isn't working—every fiber of your being wants to intervene. You have the resources to make the problem disappear. You could call the teacher, switch the team, or have them start a different project. And sometimes those interventions are appropriate. But when intervention becomes the default response to any friction your child encounters, you are systematically destroying their capacity to handle friction on their own. The same principle applies even when no specific struggle is involved. Simply living amid abundance—the private flights, the seamless logistics, the staff who handle every inconvenience—eliminates the natural exposure to problems that once developed capability without anyone having to think about it. You don't have to actively shield your children from difficulty; wealth does it automatically unless you deliberately push back.

Recall Sowell's quote, shared in chapter 4: "There are no solutions; there are only trade-offs."[2] Wealth provides comfort, opportunity, and security. Those are genuine goods. But wealth also removes the natural feedback loops that once forced children to develop capability. The trade-off is real, and pretending otherwise doesn't make it disappear.

Families who navigate this well understand that engineering an environment in which their children are required to struggle to achieve an objective is an act of love. They are not being cruel when they refuse to solve every problem. They are not being negligent by allowing their children to fail. They are doing the hard work of building human beings who can stand on their own—trees with stress wood, capable of weathering whatever storms arrive.

Think again of Viktor Frankl, writing from the depths of suffering in Nazi concentration camps. He observed that meaning could be found even in unavoidable hardship. "Everything can be taken from a man but one thing: the last of the human freedoms—to choose one's attitude in any given set of circumstances, to choose one's own way."[3] But Frankl also noted something subtler: that meaning often emerges precisely through the struggle itself, through the attitude we adopt when facing adversity. The struggle is not merely an obstacle to be endured on the way to meaning. It is frequently the source of meaning. The obstacle is the way.

This insight transforms how we think about the challenges our children face. We are not trying to minimize their suffering while they wait for the good parts of life to arrive. We are helping them discover that the struggle—engaged with the right attitude and connected to something that matters—is where much of life's richness actually lives.

The Four Quadrants

Not all struggle produces growth. And not all comfort produces decay. The relationship between friction and meaning is more nuanced than simple prescriptions allow.

JOYFUL STRUGGLE MATRIX

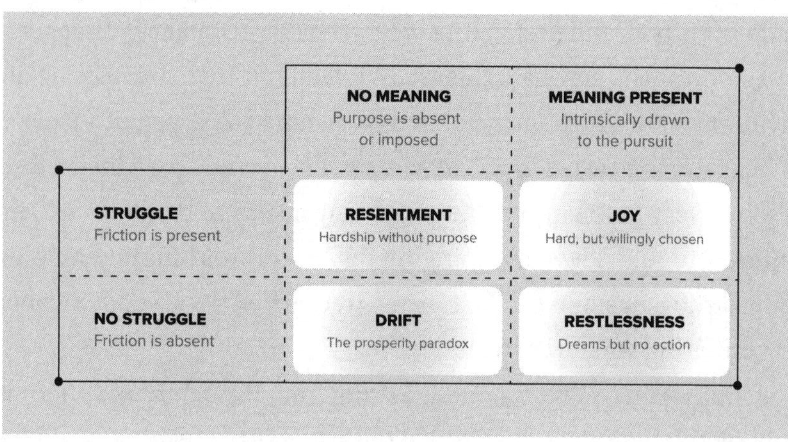

Figure 18

Consider a two-by-two matrix (see figure 18). On one axis, we have struggle, where friction is either present or absent. On the other axis, we have meaning, where purpose is either present (the child is intrinsically drawn to the pursuit) or absent (expectations are externally imposed). This gives us four quadrants, and understanding them helps diagnose what might be happening with your children.

Resentment emerges when struggle is present but meaning is absent. The child is forced to endure difficulty they never chose, for reasons never explained. Effort feels like punishment. This is the story of too many students in school who are forced to endure intellectual struggle, memorizing things they couldn't care less about, without any context for why the content should matter to them. It is the daughter dragged to piano lessons she hates, grinding through scales while dreaming of escape, or the son placed in a summer role at the family office to be "shown the ropes," grinding through tasks he finds meaningless while counting days until it ends. Over time, they learn to avoid hard things entirely, because hard things have only ever been associated with misery. The output is learned helplessness, rebellion, and an aversion to challenge that can persist for decades. (This was my story during my teen years, where I cheated for years because I resented being required to learn things I didn't care about, and I didn't find any meaning in the school struggle.)

Drift occurs when neither struggle nor meaning is present. This is the prosperity paradox we've discussed throughout this book. Money removed necessity and nothing replaced it. There's no friction, no direction, and no compelling reason to do anything in particular. Energy scatters. Consumption becomes identity. Even good kids start to rot internally if they are not needed. The output is entitlement, fragility, and what we might call *meaning insolvency*—a bankruptcy of purpose that all the family's financial wealth cannot remedy.

Restlessness appears when meaning is present but struggle is absent or avoided. These are the dreamers, the ones with big visions but no sustained friction to test those visions against reality. Taylor spent his early twenties bouncing from one big idea to the next, always tempted to jump into a new thing instead of enduring what was required to build something that offered meaning. The excitement about what could be built is genuine, but without committing to the sustained struggle required to actually build it, the person accumulates evidence for a portfolio that demonstrates that they don't finish what they start. Self-efficacy erodes even as ambition remains high. The output is serial dreaming and an imposter identity.

Joy is the quadrant we're aiming for. Here, struggle and meaning converge. The work is hard, but it's willingly chosen. The child doesn't even recognize it as struggle because they're focused on the exciting future that draws them forward. Difficulty is the price paid for something they can't not pursue. This is passion in its pure sense: to struggle for something you love.

The output of joyful struggle is self-efficacy, peak moments, and a builder identity that compounds over time. Preston experienced this on the basketball court. The practices were grueling, the competition fierce, and the injuries painful. But he was drawn to it. He wanted to be there, competing against the best, testing himself, and growing. The struggle was joyful because it was connected to something that mattered to him: a belief in who he was capable of becoming.

The key insight is that parents cannot simply add struggle to their children's lives and expect positive results. Struggle without meaning produces resentment. The work is to connect struggle to something the child *actually cares about*—to find or create environments where difficulty is in service of a purpose the child has internalized, not one imposed from outside.

Designing the Environment

You cannot engineer joyful struggle directly. You cannot force your child to find something meaningful and then mandate that they suffer productively in pursuit of it. What you can do is design environments where it becomes possible, even likely.

Preston's father engineered an environment that demanded excellence, with immediate feedback. The stakes were real. And crucially, Preston wanted to be there. He loved basketball. The system channeled that love into structured challenge. My own father took a different approach toward the same end. Throughout my childhood, he filled our home with computers—the latest technology, always available for me to explore. When I discovered an early interest in programming, those machines became my laboratory. I spent countless late nights wrestling with code, trying to build things, hunting for answers in an era before YouTube tutorials or AI made solutions easy to find. The struggle was real: hours of frustration, failed experiments, and problems I couldn't solve for days. But it was joyful struggle because the pursuit was mine. I loved technology. My father didn't force me to learn programming; he created an environment where my own curiosity could flourish, and the difficulty became the price I was willing to pay.

This is the parental art: observing what your children are drawn to, and then creating or finding environments where that interest can be pursued with appropriate rigor. The child who loves rockets might be enrolled in a robotics program where the expectations are high and the work is demanding. The child fascinated by animals might spend summers working on a relative's ranch with real responsibilities and real consequences for failure. The child drawn to entrepreneurship might be supported in starting a small venture where customers provide unfiltered feedback and market forces teach lessons no lecture could convey.

The "yes, and . . ." approach is useful here. When your child expresses interest in something, avoid saying anything like "no, but we can do this instead," as this shuts down their curiosity and signals that their interests don't matter. "Yes, and . . ." builds upon their initiative. Yes, you want to learn about horses, and let's find a way for you to actually work with them. Yes, you're interested in making videos, and here's how we might turn that into something more rigorous than just consuming content.

The environment you create should have several characteristics. First, the challenge should be real. Simulated difficulty that the child knows isn't genuine produces cynicism rather than growth. Second, the feedback should be fast. Long delays between effort and result make it hard to learn and easy to lose motivation. Third, someone outside the parent-child relationship should be invested in the outcome—a coach, a mentor, a customer, a teammate, or other adult. This adds accountability that parental expectations alone cannot provide. Fourth, the stakes should be appropriate to the child's age and capacity—high enough to matter, low enough that failure isn't catastrophic.

What you're building is a practice ground for life. The specific activity matters less than the structure around it. Basketball, music, entrepreneurship, farming—any of these and countless more can be vehicles for joyful struggle if the environment is designed well.

Naming the Mountain

Joyful struggle becomes even more powerful when it's named and referenced as part of building family culture. Lee Brower, my former business coach, shares a story from another entrepreneur he coached that drives this point home. This man, whom we'll call Jonathan, decided to take his three kids, all under nine, on a fairly rigorous mountain hike. None of the children had ever been hiking before, and Jonathan was nervous about whether they could handle such an adventure. But he hyped up how exciting it would be, and off they went with his wife alongside them.

The hike was exciting at the start; the kids were climbing over boulders, enjoying themselves as they made their way up. Then it started to rain. The boulders grew slick, and the children began slipping and sliding as they tried to scramble over them. Complaints quickly came, and the younger kids began to whine and cry. Part of Jonathan wanted to turn back. But they pressed on. And as they neared the summit, the sun broke through. At the peak, they sat together among clusters of yellow wildflowers, caught their breath, and took in the views of a beautiful vista. It was clear to everyone that the journey's struggles made the experience much more meaningful and memorable.

When Jonathan shared this story, Lee encouraged him to name the moment and share that name with his family. They called it their "Yellow Flower Moment," and it became part of their culture. As the children grow older and they face something difficult—a challenging project, a setback, or a goal that seems beyond reach—they have a reference point. Remember the yellow flowers. Remember what it felt like to want to quit, to push through anyway, and to discover what was waiting at the top. The named experience becomes part of the family's shared language, a touchstone they can return to when they need courage.

This is how peak moments function. They are not just experiences; they are anchoring contexts that shape how the family understands itself. Matt Higgins, a serial entrepreneur and guest shark on *Shark Tank*, can recall selling flowers on the streets of Queens as a ten-year-old when he needs to remember who he is and what he's capable of. Ricardo Salinas, the Mexican business icon, can recall going door to door selling honey from his beehives (also at age ten!) on the streets of Pedregal. I remember receiving my first check from a client for a website I built—the first bit of evidence that I can build things that didn't previously exist. Early experiences of purposeful struggle become the mythos around which identity forms.

PEAK MOMENTS FRAMEWORK

Figure 19

As noted in chapter 3, a peak moment is an experience in which a positive reflection is achieved in a meaningful area of life. Peak moments (see figure 19) have the power to transform our capabilities and our perspective—who we believe we are now capable of becoming. It has three components: the leap, the struggle, and the outcome. The leap is the decision to begin—to step into uncertainty, to commit to something challenging. The struggle is the difficult middle, where growth actually happens and commitment is tested. The outcome is the resolution—not necessarily success in conventional terms, but completion, the closing of a loop that began with the leap. And then, critically, comes the naming: You identify the experience, give it a label, and add it to the family's collective memory.

When you help your children accumulate named peak moments, you are building their portfolio of evidence that they can do hard things. Self-efficacy—the belief that you can produce desired outcomes through your own actions—doesn't come from being *told* you're capable. It comes from having *done* capable things. "I can do things because I've done things," as Taylor puts it. Each named peak moment adds to the evidence portfolio, making the next challenge feel more approachable. The capability compounds.

The family's role here is part documentarian, part meaning-maker. You notice when something significant has happened. You help your child see the full arc—the leap, the struggle, the outcome—rather than just the difficulty in the middle. You name it together. And you return to it whenever its lessons are relevant.

The Forge of Capability

Resilience cannot be inherited. You cannot pass down to your children the grit you developed through your own struggles simply by telling them about it. They have to build their own.

This is perhaps the hardest truth for successful parents to accept. The very qualities that enabled you to build wealth—your tolerance for risk, your ability to persevere through setbacks, your comfort with uncertainty—were forged in experiences your children will never have unless you deliberately create substitutes. The farm that taught past generations responsibility, the scarcity that forced our parents or grandparents to be resourceful, the early failures that taught us to get back up—these were not optional developmental features. They were the crucible. And you cannot simply describe the crucible to your children and expect them to emerge from the description transformed.

What you can do is build new crucibles appropriate to their circumstances. The Texas Titans. The summer as a ranch hand. The venture that might fail. The competition where there's no place to hide. The kids market where strangers are the judge. These designed struggles are not punishments or arbitrary hardships imposed to build character through various degrees of suffering. They are loving acts of environmental engineering—creating the conditions within which your children can develop the stress wood they will need to stand on their own.

The alternative is Biosphere 2: an optimized environment that produces fast growth and structural fragility. Trees that look healthy until they collapse. Children who seem fine until life's inevitable winds arrive. Each of our children deserves better. They deserve the chance to struggle joyfully toward something that matters to them, to accumulate evidence of their own capability, and to build the internal architecture that will let them weather whatever comes.

Principles

1. **Resilience cannot be inherited; it must be engineered.** The qualities that made the wealth-creating generation successful—grit, risk tolerance, perseverance—were frequently forged through experiences that abundance naturally eliminates. Children growing up in prosperity will not automatically develop these qualities. Parents must deliberately design environments where joyful struggle can occur. The goal is to create modern equivalents of the challenges that shaped previous generations, adapted to current circumstances but no less formative.
2. **Comfort is the enemy of capability. Purpose grows through productive struggle.** When difficulty is connected to something the child genuinely cares about, struggle transforms from burden to building material. The key distinction is between resentment (struggle without meaning) and joyful struggle (difficulty in service of a purpose the child has internalized). Parents cannot impose meaning, but they can observe what their children are drawn to and create rigorous pathways for pursuing those interests. Passion in its original sense—to struggle for something you love—is what we're cultivating.

Application Examples

These ideas matter most when translated from concept to concrete action. Below is a sampling of age-appropriate prompts to guide you with your children or grandchildren.

Get the full list at WealthTrapBook.com/list.

- **Ages 5–8**

  Find one physical challenge slightly beyond your child's current ability—a hike, a climbing wall, or learning to ride a bike without training wheels. When they complete it, name the experience together. Put a photo on the wall. Reference it when they face something difficult: "You can do hard things." The specific challenge matters less than the naming and reinforcement.

- **Ages 9–12**

  Identify what your child is genuinely drawn to—a sport, a craft, a subject, a skill—and find an environment where that interest can be pursued with rigor. Look for programs with high expectations, coaches who don't coddle, or peers who will push your child to improve. Be willing to let them struggle, even when you could intervene to make things easier.

- **Ages 13–17**

  Create or find opportunities for real-world struggle with real-world stakes. A summer job in a demanding environment. A competitive program where talent alone isn't enough. A venture where customers will provide unfiltered feedback. When they want to quit—and they likely will!—help them see the bigger picture without removing the difficulty. The goal is to complete the loop, to add this experience to their evidence portfolio, regardless of whether it succeeds by conventional measures.

- **Ages 18–25**

  Encourage them to put themselves in situations where they are not the most capable person in the room—new cities, challenging jobs, competitive graduate programs, start-up environments. Help them name and memorialize the peak moments as they occur, building the narrative of someone who has faced difficulty and grown through it. This becomes their origin story, the anchoring context for everything that follows.

CHAPTER 10

Experiments and Feedback Loops

James (name changed for privacy) grew up in an Irving, Texas, tract home watching his father build an oil and gas company from nothing. His dad was the son of a truck driver and a teacher, a Texas A&M engineer who started at thirty with two small children and the audacity to believe he could value wells better than anyone else at the courthouse auctions. There was no opulence in James's childhood—money was tight, and his father was largely absent, grinding to build the business. The wealth didn't arrive until James was away at college. By then, he had already internalized what it took to get there: a lifetime of hard work, a lot of luck, and a father who created real value by extracting energy that larger companies had left unexploited.

Now the family office is stable and compounding. Luxuries they never before dreamed of are available and enjoyed. But James carries that blue-collar origin story with him, reinforced by his wife's family heritage of risk-taking ranchers. They know what it's like to sacrifice and struggle, but how do they pass on that perspective to their kids? "We fly on private planes sometimes," James shared, "and what we think about is, how do we not raise brats?"[1]

Their oldest daughter was six when they decided to let her try selling lemonade. What happened next was electric. They didn't buy a kit or simplify the process. The daughter had to plan it—figure out what supplies she needed, make the lemonade from scratch, draw the signs, and set up the stand. The work stretched over days. There were moments of boredom, moments of frustration, and moments when the project seemed like more trouble than it was worth. Then the cars started pulling over.

"She was on fire with it," James recalled. "She was a natural salesperson. We realized that this is what we need to feed." He watched his six-year-old collect money from strangers, thank them, pour cups, and make change. She was beaming. The feedback was immediate: People wanted what she had made. They were willing to pay for it. She had created something of value, and the world was reflecting that value back to her. "I said that to her," James explained. "You made people's day really enjoyable with this cup of lemonade. And look what you got in return for it. When you make money, you've added value for somebody."

A lemonade stand. The most clichéd childhood business imaginable. But James recognized what was actually happening: His daughter had completed a full feedback loop. She had hypothesized that people might want lemonade, created value by making it, faced the constraint of actually setting up and running a stand, committed to the work even when it was tedious, and then debriefed naturally afterward as the family discussed what had happened. The loop closed. The learning was embodied. And his daughter walked away with something more valuable than the dollars in her hand: evidence that she could do something real in the world.

The Power of Tight Loops

Children learn best when they do something that matters and see results fast. Consider the alternative: A child is told they should work hard in school because someday, perhaps fifteen years from now, the accumulated knowledge and credentials will help them get a good job. The feedback loop stretches over more than a decade. The connection between today's effort and eventual outcome is abstract, distant, and mediated by countless variables the child cannot control. Is it any wonder that motivation flags? That the work feels meaningless? That so many students become, like I did, resentful of the schooling process?

Now consider the simple lemonade stand. The loop closes in an afternoon. Effort connects directly to outcome. The child makes a choice, takes an action, and immediately sees what happens. If the sign is unclear, customers don't stop. If the lemonade is too sour, people won't buy a second cup. If the stand is positioned poorly, traffic passes by. Every variable is a lesson, and every lesson arrives in real time.

When we aim to engineer an environment that offers joyful struggle in pursuit of something great, this is the structure we ought to create: experiments with fast feedback that teach children how to create value, take risks, and iterate based on results. The specific vehicle matters less than the loop itself. Lemonade stands, farmers markets, door-to-door sales, lawn care services, coding projects, YouTube channels—any of these can work if the structure is right.

Fast feedback leads to quick iteration and improvement. I see this regularly at our Kids Markets events across the country, where kids ages five to seventeen sell real products for real money, interact with customers, and compete alongside peers (see KidsMarkets.com). Sometimes the learning happens between markets: A participant shows up with cans of soda and bags of chips, while the booth next door features a custom boba drink station, and the kid down the aisle is selling homemade cinnamon rolls. The soda-and-chips entrepreneur will sell little that day, but they'll leave with something more valuable than revenue—a clear picture of what customers actually want. They almost always return with a dramatically improved offering, inspired by what they observed in their competition. Other times, the learning happens within minutes. A child selling cookies notices that another young entrepreneur a few booths over is moving far more brownies—and realizes the difference isn't the product but the approach. That kid is standing in front of the booth rather than sitting behind it, holding a tray of free samples, actively engaging passersby. The cookie seller takes action immediately: stands up, steps forward, and starts offering tastes. Sales increase before the market ends. This is the power of tight feedback loops in an environment with real stakes and visible peers. No lecture about salesmanship or customer engagement could teach what ten minutes of observation and imitation accomplish.

Experiments Within Epics

The lemonade stand worked for James's daughter partly because she was intrinsically interested in it—she loved lemonade and was excited about selling it—and partly because the loop was appropriately sized for her age and capacity. But there's a third element that makes experiments genuinely developmental rather than merely entertaining: They need to connect to something larger.

Taylor calls this framing "experiments within epics." An experiment without context is just an activity. An experiment that connects to a bigger vision of who the child is becoming, or what the family is building together, becomes part of a meaningful trajectory. The lemonade stand, therefore, isn't just a fun Saturday project; it's the beginning of learning how business works, how value creation functions, and how this child might eventually contribute to the family's legacy as a builder.

This doesn't mean burdening a six-year-old with the weight of generational expectations. It means that parents hold the larger frame even when children can't yet see it. When the daughter asks if she can do another lemonade stand, the parents say yes—and privately note that this is part of her developing a builder identity. When she's older, they might talk more explicitly about how these early experiments connect to larger questions about who she wants to become. For now, the framing lives mostly in the parents' minds, guiding how they support and extend what their children initiate.

Thirteen-year-old Taylor's idea to do a radio ad was an experiment. He walked into the local radio station in a suit, shaking with nerves, to buy airtime. His dad's entire contribution was writing a check and providing a ride. And the commercial itself was a failure by conventional measures—it didn't sell superchargers. But framed within the epic of Taylor learning to take initiative, face discomfort, and operate in adult environments, the experiment was a profound success. It became anchoring context for everything that followed—evidence that he could put himself in uncomfortable situations and produce something real.

The experiment failed. The epic advanced. Both can be true simultaneously.

The Meaning Experiments Framework

If you want to move from good intentions to actual practice, it helps to have a structure. The following framework offers one way to design experiments that build your children's capacity for agency and initiative. It has five stages that form a cycle (see figure 20). Each time through the loop, the child starts from a higher position—more capability, more confidence, and more evidence of what they can do.

MEANING EXPERIMENTS FRAMEWORK

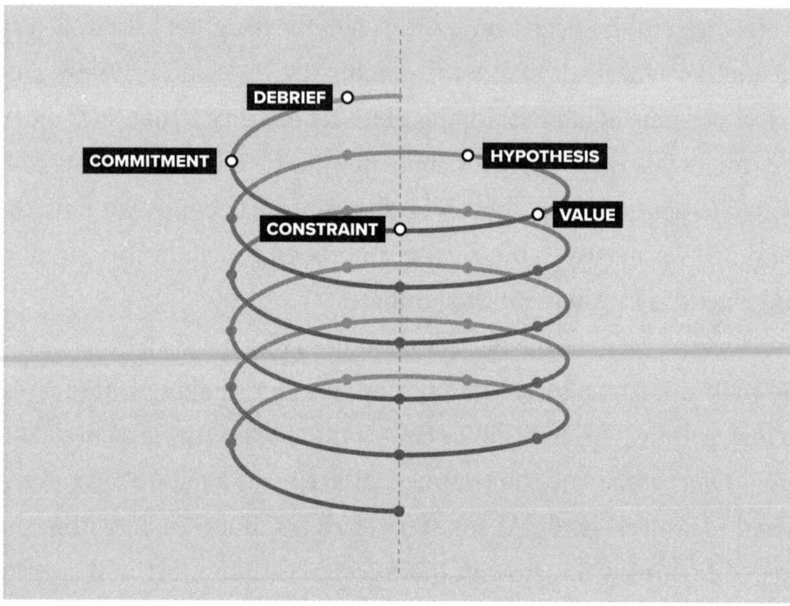

Figure 20

Hypothesis

Every experiment begins with a belief about value creation. The hypothesis needn't be sophisticated. For a young child, it might be: "I think people will buy my lemonade." For a teenager, it might be: "I think I can build an audience for videos about this topic I'm interested in." For a young adult, it might be: "I think this business idea solves a real problem people will pay to fix."

The parental role at this stage is to help the child articulate what they think might work, and for whom. Who is the audience? What value do you think you can create for them? Why would they want what you're offering? These questions don't require formal answers, but asking them helps the child think beyond "I want to do this thing" to "Here's why this thing might matter to someone else."

The hypothesis should be attached to something the child is genuinely drawn to. If you try to impose an experiment on a topic the child doesn't care about, you're back in the resentment quadrant from the previous chapter—struggle without meaning. The "yes, and . . ." approach applies here: When your child expresses interest in something, build upon it by helping them formulate a hypothesis about how that interest might create value.

Value

The second stage asks: What specific value will this create, and for whom? This forces concreteness. It's one thing for a child to say he wants to start a lawn care business. It's another to say, "I'll make Mrs. Johnson's life easier by mowing her lawn every week so she doesn't have to worry about it."

For younger children, value might be as simple as knowing that people get thirsty, so they may want a refreshing drink. For older children and young adults, the value proposition can become more sophisticated. But at every age, the exercise of articulating value—rather than just describing an activity—begins to build the mental habits of a creator rather than a consumer.

Constraint

This is the most important stage, and the one parents most often skip. An experiment without constraints is just a daydream. The constraint defines the boundaries within which the experiment will run: how long, how much, what scope, and what counts as completion.

For example, if your child expresses an interest in skiing, you might sign her up for lessons. The constraint is that determining if she might find passion in skiing will involve multiple lessons—and she has to complete them all, even if she hates it after the first few. That's the experiment: to fully understand if skiing is something she'll find passion in. The constraint forces commitment. It prevents the premature abandonment that turns every experiment into a fragment, every interest into a passing fancy.

For James's daughter, the constraint was implicit: They were going to do this lemonade stand on Saturday, and that meant completing all the preparation beforehand. For an older child starting a more substantial venture, constraints might include: three months and $500 to test an idea; completing a project even if the initial approach isn't working; or having to serve at least ten customers before evaluating whether a project is worth continuing.

The constraint creates a meaningful pursuit from which it is hard to exit. When you've committed publicly, when someone else is depending on you, when you've invested resources that can't be recovered—these create healthy pressure to see things through. Without constraints, children (and adults) tend to abandon experiments at the first sign of difficulty, which means they never learn what's on the other side of the struggle.

Commitment

The fourth stage makes the experiment real by involving someone outside the parent-child relationship. This might be a coach, a customer, a mentor, a teammate, a community partner, or even just a public declaration on social media. The point is to create accountability that parental expectations alone cannot provide.

When Taylor called capital for his first venture fund, he had a fiduciary responsibility to his LPs. He used the capital from his early investors to invest in his first three deals, so he couldn't give them their money back. He had to fill out the rest of the portfolio to provide sufficient diversification for existing investors, so he had to raise more capital from new investors. The commitment created a structure from which exit was genuinely costly. There was no going back.

For children, commitment might mean: telling their friends about the venture, signing up customers who are expecting service, joining a team where others depend on them, or entering a competition with a fixed date. The external commitment adds stakes. It transforms "I'm trying this" into "People are counting on me."

Debrief

The final stage closes the loop by reflecting on what happened. This is where learning crystallizes. Without a debrief, the experience remains unprocessed—feelings without frameworks, outcomes without understanding.

The debrief has several components. First, identify the gap between the expected and actual outcomes. Taylor's commercial didn't sell superchargers. James's daughter's lemonade stand may have made $23 instead of $50. The project took twice as long as estimated. This book took longer to write than initially planned. These gaps are data, not failures.

Second, ask what the child learned about themselves. What surprised them? What was harder than expected? What came naturally? The point is self-knowledge—building an increasingly accurate understanding of one's own capabilities, interests, and areas for growth.

Third, ask what should change next time. This forward orientation is crucial. The debrief isn't just an autopsy of a completed experiment; *it's the pre-brief for the next one*. What would you do differently? What new hypothesis does this suggest?

Finally, note any skills that were acquired or leveled up. The experiment might have failed by its stated objective while succeeding wildly in terms of capability development. Taylor's radio commercial didn't sell products, but it taught him that he could walk into a professional environment, pitch something to adults, and produce an actual broadcast. That skill acquisition was the real output.

The debrief connects directly back to forming the next hypothesis. What you learned informs what you try next. The cycle continues, each iteration building on the last, the child's capacity compounding over time.

The Gap and the Gain

One of the most powerful perspective shifts you can offer your children, particularly when debriefing and creating new experiments, is teaching them to measure progress by growth rather than by distance from perfection.

GAP AND GAIN FRAMEWORK

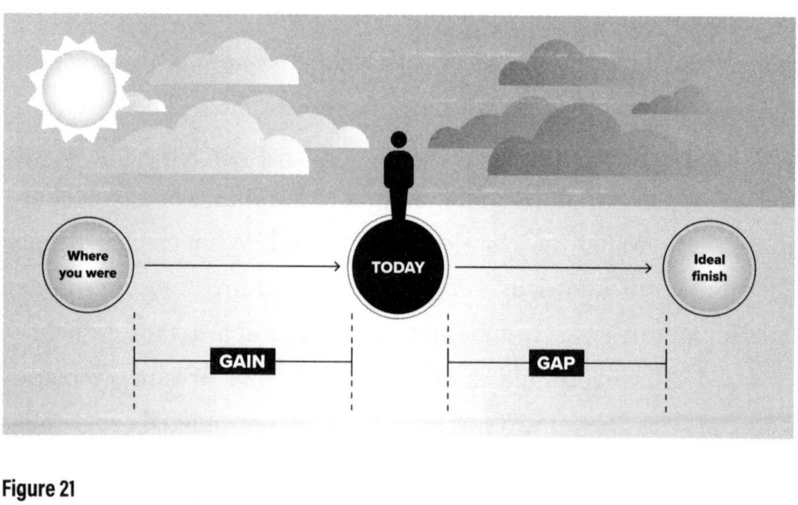

Figure 21

This contrast is taught by Dan Sullivan with what he calls "the Gap and the Gain" (see figure 21). At any given moment, you can measure yourself against your ideal (the perfect version of what you're trying to achieve), or you can measure yourself against where you started. Measuring against the ideal puts you in "the gap": No matter how much progress you've made, you're still falling short of the (ever-changing) ideal, and the gap feels discouraging. Measuring against your starting point, by contrast, puts you in "the gain": You can see how far you've come, and the progress feels energizing.

Children naturally tend toward the gap, especially high achievers. The lemonade stand made $23, but she wanted to make $50, so she's disappointed. The project took two months, but he wanted to finish in one, so he feels like he fell behind. The video got two hundred views, but she was hoping for thousands, so she's discouraged. This approach becomes self-limiting as you focus more on what you still lack than on what you actually achieved.

Parents can help by redirecting attention to the gain. Making $23 is better than zero. Completion of a project, and all the learning that came with it, is worth celebrating. Two hundred people watching something you created is nothing to sneeze at. The progress is real. The gain is real. And recognizing the gain builds the confidence to attempt the next experiment.

To be clear, this isn't toxic positivity or participation trophies for everyone. The gap is not something to simply ignore; there's value in understanding how far you have to go to achieve genuine excellence. But for children who are developing their sense of agency, living perpetually in the gap is demoralizing. The gain provides the emotional fuel to keep going. New experiments are energized when we reflect on the progress from past ones.

After each experiment, make the gain explicit by helping your children see the full arc: where they were when they started, the struggle they navigated, and where they are now. This is the material from which self-efficacy is built. Not the *belief* that everything they do is wonderful, but the *evidence*—concrete, specific, undeniable—that they can take action in the world and produce real results.

Building the Evidence Portfolio

We can make it easier for our children to live in the gain by creating experiments that expand their evidence portfolio—the accumulated proof that they can do things, because they have done things. This portfolio is the foundation of self-efficacy. When your daughter faces a daunting challenge at sixteen, she can reach back to the lemonade stand at six, the kids market at nine, the summer business at twelve, or the serious venture at fifteen. Each completed experiment adds to the weight of evidence. Each named peak moment becomes anchoring context for future pursuits. The portfolio compounds.

More than that, the portfolio becomes the raw material for their own origin story. Matt Higgins selling flowers on the streets of Queens. Ricardo Salinas selling honey at ten years old. Taylor shaking in a suit in a conference room at thirteen. These early experiments didn't seem momentous at the time. They were just a kid trying something, facing some discomfort, and producing some result. But they became the stories these builders tell about themselves—the anchoring contexts that inform how they understand who they are and what they're capable of.

Your role as a parent is partly to create opportunities for experiments, and partly to help memorialize them. Take photos. Tell the story at family dinners. Reference the early experiments when later challenges arise. "Remember your first kids market, when you were terrified to talk to customers? Look at you now." "You know how hard you struggled to get your first customers? Now you have a thousand!" The connection between past evidence and present capability is what transforms isolated experiences into a coherent identity. But we're easily forgetful and naturally forward-looking, which is why we so often fall into the gap. Building a family culture of remembering is key to building a gain-centered evidence portfolio.

A culture without artifacts is not a culture at all. The named experiments, the photos on the wall, the stories told and retold—these are the artifacts of your family's builder culture. They make visible what would otherwise fade into the general blur of childhood. They create the shared language that gives your family's values concrete meaning.

The Human Capital Profit

We must stress this point: The point of children's experiments is not financial profit. A lemonade stand that makes $23 hasn't failed because it didn't produce enough revenue to offset expenses. A teenage venture that breaks even hasn't underperformed because it didn't generate wealth. Kids don't fail if their idea falls flat and costs money.

The profit we're after is human capital profit. Each microventure is R&D on the child's own strengths and interests. Each experiment generates data about who they are and who they might become. The financial outcomes are almost beside the point; what matters is the development of capability, confidence, and agency. We're investing in people, not products and services.

James's own developmental experiments involved working as a hospital orderly cleaning up after surgeries, doing manual labor in the oil fields, and interning at the Department of Labor in DC. None of these produced financial returns for his family. But each generated learning: about himself, about the world, about what he did and didn't want. The miserable hospital job taught him that he could handle discomfort. The oil field work showed him what hard physical labor actually felt like. The DC internship revealed how little actually got done in bureaucratic environments. These insights compounded into the person he eventually became.

And seeing what his own evidence portfolio has done for him has led him to begin thinking of similar experiments for his own children. His wife's cousin runs a ranch in Oklahoma. "I'm going to send my kids up there," he told us. "They're going to spend two weeks being a cowboy with Uncle Angus." The ranch experience won't be a vacation. It's an experiment—a deliberate exposure to difficulty, independence, and responsibility in an environment where the stakes are real and the feedback is immediate.

This is the scaffolding that families of builders provide: not the answers, but the structure within which children can discover their own answers. We encourage our kids to launch experiments that entail joyful struggle. (To encourage another is to, quite literally, *give them courage.*) Your children will eventually inherit whatever financial capital your family has built. But the more important inheritance—the one that determines whether they'll leverage that stored energy wisely or be consumed by it—is the evidence portfolio they've accumulated along the way. Every experiment you help them launch, every loop you help them close, every debrief where you help them extract meaning from experience: these are deposits into a human capital account far more valuable than any trust fund.

The money will come to them whether they're ready or not. The evidence that they can build, create, and contribute? That only comes from having actually done it.

Principles

1. **Experimentation is the antidote to entitlement.** When children learn to create value through repeated cycles of hypothesis, constraint, commitment, and debrief, they develop an identity as

someone who produces rather than consumes. Each completed experiment adds evidence to the portfolio of their capability. Entitlement becomes structurally difficult to maintain when you have years of experience demonstrating that value must be created before it can be captured. The experiments need not be grand, but they must be real, with genuine stakes and feedback from sources outside the family.

2. **Short feedback loops turn curiosity into confidence.** The power of experiments lies in the speed at which effort connects to outcome. When a child tries something and immediately sees what happens, they learn in ways that no lecture or delayed consequence can match. Fast loops maintain motivation, generate rapid iteration, and build the pattern recognition that eventually becomes judgment. Families should bias toward experiments that can be completed quickly, reserving longer-duration ventures for children who have already built confidence through many smaller loops.

Application Examples

These ideas matter most when translated from concept to concrete action. Below is a sampling of age-appropriate prompts to guide you with your children or grandchildren.

Get the full list at WealthTrapBook.com/list.

- **Ages 5–8**

  Help your child identify something they could make or do that someone else might want. It could be lemonade, baked goods, handmade cards, or a simple act of service. Walk through the hypothesis together: Who might want this, and why? Set a constraint: We'll try this one time on Saturday. After the experiment, debrief: What happened? What did you learn? What would you do differently?

- **Ages 9–12**

  Expand the scope and introduce external commitment. A kids market booth, a regular lawn care customer, a craft sale with advertised inventory, and so on. The constraint should extend over weeks rather than hours. Someone outside the family should be involved—a customer, a mentor, or an event organizer. The debrief should explicitly name what skills were acquired and what the child learned about themselves. Begin intentionally building the evidence portfolio: photos, written reflections, and artifacts to reference later.

- **Ages 13–17**

  Here the experiments should have higher stakes, whether an actual business with overhead and risk of failure, a creative project with public exposure, or a competitive program where performance matters. Parents can provide scaffolding—access to capital, introductions, or ideas—without removing the genuine difficulty. The debrief should help your teen see how this experiment connects to larger questions about who they want to become.

- **Ages 18–25**

  Support ventures that are genuinely hard to exit. Businesses with customers depending on them. Commitments that can't be easily unwound. Geographic moves that force independence. The parental role shifts toward being a thought partner rather than a supervisor. Help them frame experiments within epics—connecting current efforts to the larger trajectory of who they're becoming. Celebrate the completion of loops, regardless of conventional success or failure. The portfolio by now should be substantial; help them see the pattern in it, the emerging identity of someone who experiments, learns, and grows.

CHAPTER 11

Contagious Self-Actualization

Melissa Osborn keeps track of three hundred people. As the head of the Coors family office (and a fifth-generation member herself), she manages the governance and administration for descendants spanning seven generations—from Adolph Coors, who stowed away on a ship to America as an orphan, worked his way across the country, and built a brewery in Golden, Colorado, all the way down to great-great-great-grandchildren scattered across the globe, some of whom have never set foot in Colorado and don't share the Coors name.

The math is unforgiving. When Adolph died, his six children inherited the business. When those children had children, the ownership divided again. And again. And again. By now, the financial distributions that once represented life-changing wealth have been diluted across so many branches that they're meaningful but not necessarily transformative. More importantly, the story itself—the orphan who built an empire through relentless hard work—has grown distant. For some family members who live in South Africa or Europe, Adolph is an abstraction. A name on a document. A sepia-toned photograph in an email from the family office. "The question I keep asking myself," Melissa told me, "is how do we create new first generations? How do we spin off builders?"[1]

She's watched what happens when the connective tissue weakens. Some branches of the family have drifted entirely, their members living comfortable lives with no particular sense of connection to the family legacy. Others may expect distributions without contribution. And a few—a precious few—have caught something. They've built businesses of their own. They've become, in Melissa's words, first generations in their own right.

Her sister Christi is one of them.

Christi and her husband bought a winery in Napa. They didn't need to. The family resources could have funded a leisurely life of wine consumption rather than wine production. But something in Christi compelled her to build. When she tells the story of her winery, she connects it to Adolph: "I come from a family that's been in the beer business for a long time, that survived and succeeded through hard work and dedication. Those are the ethics and morals and values that I hold, and that we exhibit in the work we do at our winery."

Here's what fascinates Melissa: Christi's children are growing up watching their mother build something. They see her work. They see her struggle. They see her make decisions and live with consequences. And because they're witnessing transformation in real time—not hearing about it in a story from 150 years ago—they're absorbing it in a way that no family newsletter or periodic reunion could accomplish. "She's a builder," Melissa observed.

Christi's kids, according to Melissa, don't really associate with being Coors family members. And yet, paradoxically, those children may end up more connected to Adolph's spirit than cousins who still bear the Coors name but have never built anything themselves.

This is the puzzle at the heart of legacy: How do values travel across generations when the people who embodied those values are long dead and the financial resources that once enforced discipline have been diluted into comfort?

The answer, we've come to believe, is contagion.

Purpose and Proximity

Self-actualization is contagious. When one family member pursues meaning with visible commitment—when they struggle, grow, and transform in ways that others can observe—something shifts in the family system. The pursuit becomes aspirational. Replicable. Possible.

This is different from inspiration at a distance. Hearing about great-great-grandfather's hardships is interesting. Watching your sister build a winery is activating. The difference is proximity—not just physical closeness, but the ability to observe the microstages of transformation as they happen.

Taylor describes it this way: "We can't become what we don't have the opportunity to observe. And the inverse is true—we will become what we regularly have the opportunity to observe." We are mimicking machines. Children mimic parents. Siblings mimic siblings. Cousins mimic cousins. The question is which behaviors are available to be mimicked, and whether mimicry leads toward building or drift.

The contagion model has a specific structure. It begins with signal: Someone in the family starts pursuing something meaningful, and that pursuit generates observable evidence. New disciplines. Changed routines. Creative output. Visible progress. A kind of locked-in calm that replaces the anxious drift of purposelessness.

Next comes legibility: Those signals must be interpretable by others in the system. If everyone retreats to their rooms and pursues private projects that no one discusses, there's nothing to catch. The transformation has to be visible—shared at family dinners, referenced in conversations, made concrete through the family's operating system of communication and ritual.

Then mimicry: Others in the family, consciously or unconsciously, begin adopting elements of what they've observed. A younger sibling starts waking up early. A cousin asks questions about how the business works. Someone who had been drifting starts talking about an idea they want to pursue.

Finally, multiplication: The original builder's transformation activates others, who then become contagious themselves. The network effect compounds. What began with one person pursuing meaning becomes a family culture where building is normal, expected, and mutually reinforced.

THE CONTAGION EFFECT

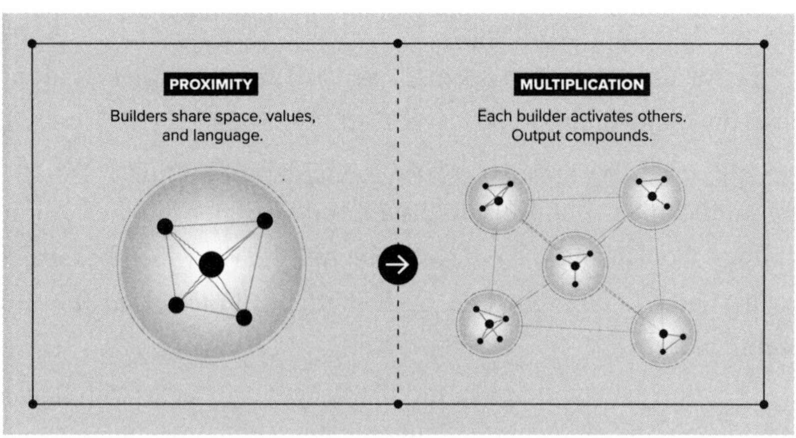

Figure 22

This is what happened with the PayPal mafia—the group of early employees and founders who worked together at PayPal in the late

1990s and early 2000s, including Peter Thiel, Elon Musk, Luke Nosek, Scott Banister, and others. After PayPal was acquired by eBay, these individuals went on to found or lead Tesla, SpaceX, LinkedIn, YouTube, Yelp, Palantir, and dozens of other consequential companies. Observers sometimes wonder, "What was in the water at PayPal?" How did one company produce so many builders?

The answer is contagion. These people worked in close proximity during a period of intense building; this is where contagion incubates most effectively (see figure 22). They observed each other solving hard problems, taking risks, and recovering from failures. They developed a shared vocabulary for what excellence looked like. When they left PayPal, they carried that contagion with them—and they sought out environments where similar dynamics could continue. Many of them collaborated with one another and invested in each other's companies. And their habits, ideas, and perspectives infected those around them at their new companies. The network effects multiplied.

Most families will never produce a PayPal mafia. But the same dynamics apply at smaller scales. One cousin building a successful business changes what other cousins believe is possible. One sibling transforming their health and discipline creates a new reference point to be mimicked. One parent visibly struggling to build something—rather than coasting on inherited resources—gives children permission to struggle themselves.

The family doesn't need everyone to self-actualize at once. It needs one builder to go first.

The Timing of Contagion

There's a counterintuitive truth about when contagion spreads. You might assume that the most contagious family member is the one who has already succeeded—the cousin who sold their company, the uncle whose investments paid off, or the parent who previously built something enduring. But research on actual disease contagion suggests otherwise: People are often most contagious just before and just after symptoms appear, not at the peak of illness.

The same seems true of self-actualization. The family member who IPO'd their company ten years ago and now lives comfortably is less contagious than the one who is currently in the messy middle of building something. The transformation that's happening now—visible, uncertain, and incomplete—is what activates mimicry. Others can see themselves in the struggle. They can imagine taking similar steps. The outcome is still unknown, which makes the whole endeavor feel possible rather than exceptional or anomalous.

This has practical implications. Families that only celebrate completed achievements—the successful exit, the finished project, the goal attained—may actually reduce contagion. The achievement seems too distant, too polished, or too much the product of talents others don't possess. But families that make the *process* visible—the early mornings, the failed attempts, the pivots and iterations—create more opportunities for mimicry. Others can copy the inputs even when they can't guarantee the outputs.

Taylor experienced this in his own family after getting sober. The transformation was visible and ongoing. Family members watched him develop new disciplines, adopt new routines, and become a different version of himself. And that visibility, combined with his willingness to be vulnerable about the process, made him a magnet for others who were struggling with their own challenges. The contagion spread through openness, not through polished success stories.

Building the Mesh Network

Here is where the architecture of family relationships becomes critical.

Consider the different ways a family can be structured. In network topology terms, there are several models (see figure 23). A ring network passes information sequentially—you talk to your sister, who talks to your cousin, who talks to your uncle; meaningful relationships are structured linearly, with only certain family members being close to and communicating with others. The message degrades with each transmission, like a game of telephone. A star network has one central node—perhaps a patriarch or matriarch—through whom most communication flows. Everyone talks to Mom; no one talks to each other with vulnerability and earnestness. A hierarchical network looks like a corporate org chart: parents to children, with clear lines of authority and limited lateral connection.

NETWORK TOPOLOGY

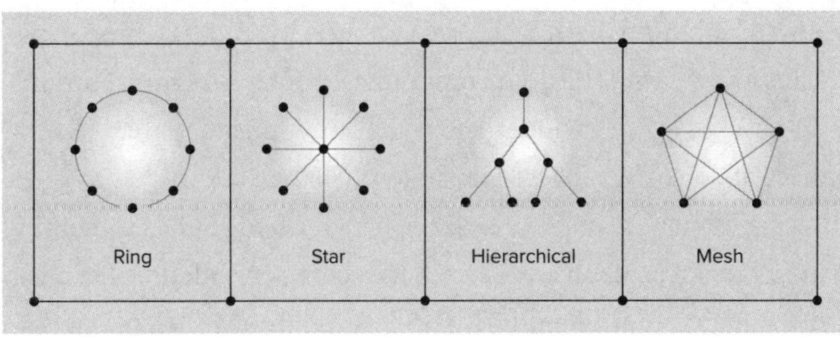

Figure 23

Each of these structures is fragile in its own way. The ring breaks if any single connection fails. The star collapses when the central node disappears—which is why so many families fall apart when the parents die. The hierarchical model requires constant succession planning, because the whole structure depends on someone being at the top and running the show.

The alternative is a mesh network, in which each node connects to multiple other nodes. There's no single point of failure. Information flows through many channels. If one connection weakens, others compensate. The network is antifragile by design.

Most families default to a star or hierarchical structure without thinking about it. The parents are the hub; the children are spokes. When the parents age and eventually die, the children often discover they have no direct, deep relationships with each other—only relationships mediated through the now-absent hub. The family scatters. This is one reason why shirtsleeves-to-shirtsleeves happens in three generations: The first generation builds and serves as the hub, the second generation orbits that hub without developing their own connections, and the third generation inherits resources without relationships.

A mesh network family looks different. Siblings have direct, substantive relationships with each other—not simply through the parents. Cousins know each other and communicate independently. The family operating system includes rituals and rhythms that create lateral connection, not just vertical transmission. When one node struggles, others can provide support directly. When one node builds something exciting, others can observe and catch the contagion without it having to filter through a central authority or degrade through telephone-like transmission between disconnected individuals.

This structure is what makes self-actualization contagious rather than isolated. In a star network, Christi, building her winery, would be known only to those who maintained a connection to the central hub. In a mesh network, that transformation ripples outward through multiple channels, reaching family members who might be activated by what they observe.

The sequoia trees of California, among the largest on earth, illustrate this principle in nature and offer a contrast to the Biosphere 2 example from chapter 9. Unlike many large trees, sequoias don't develop deep taproots. Their root systems are surprisingly shallow—rarely extending more than a few feet down despite the trees growing over 300 feet tall. What keeps them standing isn't depth but breadth: Sequoia roots spread outward up to 150 feet and interlock with the root systems of neighboring trees. They hold each other up. A single sequoia in isolation would be vulnerable to any strong wind. A grove of sequoias, roots intertwined, becomes nearly impossible to topple. They become antifragile—a natural mesh network.

Families that want to transmit builder values across generations need to think like a sequoia grove. The question isn't just how deep your relationship is with each child, but how interconnected the entire network can become.

The Culture of Coaching

A mesh network requires a culture of peer coaching. This isn't coaching in the formal sense of hiring a professional to provide structured guidance. It's something more organic: a cultural willingness to play small roles in each other's transformations. To offer perspective when asked. To connect people with opportunities. To reflect value back when you see someone making progress. To think about others as a break from the exhausting work of thinking about yourself.

Taylor first experienced this in Alcoholics Anonymous, where a culture of mutual support is structurally embedded in the program. Members sponsor other members. They call each other to check in. They share what they're going through, not because they need answers but because articulating struggle to another person provides its own kind of clarity. And crucially, the help flows in both directions: You might be far ahead in one dimension of life while struggling in another, which means you're simultaneously coaching and being coached. Alcoholics Anonymous is effectively a decentralized mesh network that is powered by living in constant consultation with other alcoholics through the shared language of the 12 Steps. The result? Recovery becomes contagious.

In a family context, this begins with the development of a shared language (as discussed in chapter 7) and a shared sense of belonging to the family's directionality of purpose (discussed in chapter 6). This is the basis for forming a family's mesh network (or the culture of coaching). Individuals participating in the network intuitively understand that when they transmit value, they become more valuable. This notion is reinforced through the shared language that true wealth is our ability to create value for others, not as altruism per se, but as a mutually beneficial system of support. In practice, this looks like a genuine interest in each other's pursuits—substantive engagement rather than performative cheerleading. When your niece mentions she's thinking about starting a business, you don't just say "that's nice"—you ask questions, offer to introduce her to someone who's done something similar, and follow up a month later to see how it's going. When your brother-in-law is going through a career transition, you make time to listen—not to give advice, but to help him hear his own thinking more clearly. You transmit value through the network.

This coaching culture enables the mesh network to function. Without it, you might have the structure of many connections but none of the substance. With it, every relationship becomes a potential channel for contagion—a pathway through which the pursuit of meaning can spread.

Farewell, Succession

Traditional family governance obsesses over succession. Who will lead the family office? Who will take over the business? Who will be the next patriarch or matriarch? These questions assume a hierarchical structure in which authority must be passed from one person to another, with all the fragility that entails.

A mesh network doesn't need succession in the traditional sense. It has an emergent order instead.

At any given moment, certain nodes in the network will be more central than others. Someone will be particularly active in connecting people. Someone else will generate energy by building a project that others are watching. Another might be the chief coach for a period—someone who takes a keen interest in others' lives and can offer meaningful support. These informal leadership positions arise naturally from engagement, not from title or inheritance. And they shift over time. The person who was central five years ago may have stepped back; someone else has stepped forward.

This is similar to how a pack of cyclists drafts on a long ride, or how birds fly in V-formation. The person (or bird) at the front bears the most wind resistance and does the most work. When they tire, they pull back, and someone else rotates to the front. The pack moves faster together than any individual could alone, and leadership constantly shifts based on who has capacity in the moment. No one "succeeds" to the front position; it emerges from the dynamics of the group.

For families, this means investing less energy in identifying and anointing the next generation of leaders within a fragile hierarchical structure, and more in building a network where leadership emerges naturally. It means creating connections across branches and generations so that when a natural leader appears—someone who is building, connecting, creating—the network can form around them without requiring formal transfer of authority. Hierarchy anoints; mesh networks adapt.

This is, frankly, a relief. The succession question haunts many wealthy families, particularly when the obvious candidates aren't so obvious. Multiple children with different strengths; cousins with competing visions; no clear heir apparent. In a hierarchical model, this ambiguity is a crisis. In a mesh model, it's expected. The network will sort itself out if it's antifragile. Mesh networks with self-actualization contagions floating freely between individuals are the best structure to achieve that goal.

Engineering the Environment

You cannot manufacture this form of contagion. You cannot force one family member to be inspired by another's transformation. But you can engineer environments where contagion becomes more likely.

Steve Jobs understood this at Pixar. When designing the company's headquarters, he insisted on a central atrium around which all key functions—lobby, cafeteria, mailboxes, meeting rooms, and more—would be clustered. The goal was to facilitate contagion by creating collisions between individuals. People from different departments, working on different projects, would constantly bump into each other throughout an ordinary day. Ed Catmull, Pixar's cofounder, later described the building as "Steve's own movie"[2]—a deliberate environmental design intended to shape culture and catalyze creativity.

Let's consider a natural environment with similar collisions. Coral reefs are among the most diverse ecosystems on the planet, despite occupying a tiny fraction of ocean space. Why? Density and interaction. Species are packed together, constantly encountering each other, borrowing and reinventing each other's innovations through symbiosis and co-adaptation. The reef's structure creates what scientists call the "adjacent possible"—opportunities that only emerge when diverse entities interact in close proximity. A fish alone in open water has little to mimic. A fish in a reef, surrounded by thousands of other species, has endless niches to explore. Being surrounded by diverse ideas and opportunities increases both the frequency and the potency of contagion.

Homes aren't coral reefs or Pixar-level facilities, but families can still make choices that increase density and interaction. Regular gatherings that bring together different branches. Communication systems that make transformation visible across the network. Shared projects that require collaboration and the development of a shared language. Investment structures that give family members reasons to engage with each other's work. The Coors family does a reunion every five years; Melissa wishes it were more often, so she's building digital infrastructure to create more connection in the interim. These are environmental choices that increase the odds of contagion. Engineer the system, and the ideas will spread more effectively.

The goal is to maximize observation with understanding—the ability to see what others are doing in enough depth to actually learn from it and be activated by it. Surface-level updates ("Christi bought a winery") don't spread contagion. Deep visibility ("Here's how Christi is thinking about building her brand, here are the struggles she's facing, here's what she's learning. Come visit!") does.

What You Can—and Cannot—Control

Once you implement what we've discussed in previous chapters—the family operating system, the designed environments for joyful struggle, the experiments with feedback loops—then you will have done what can be done. You will have built the conditions for contagion. What you cannot do is guarantee any particular outcome.

This is important to understand because many parents approach family legacy as a control problem. "If I just implement the right system, hire the right advisors, and create the right incentives, my children will become the people I hope they become." But human beings are not machines, and family systems are not simply engineering problems. You can increase probabilities, sure. But you cannot determine outcomes.

A cold is contagious, but not everyone catches it. You can be in close proximity to someone sick and remain healthy. The same is true of self-actualization. You can create a family where building is normal, where transformation is visible, and where the mesh network hums with connection and mutual support—and yet still have a child or grandchild who chooses drift over building. That is their choice to make. They are not failed products of a factory; they are autonomous agents writing their own stories. And everyone deserves the dignity to travel their own path.

Here is where you let yourself off the hook. Once you have engineered the environment, built a family operating system, and modeled transformation, you step back a bit and let the contagion spread—or not—according to dynamics you cannot fully control. The family's job is to optimize conditions, not to manufacture outcomes.

This is ultimately why we emphasize meaning over achievement. If the goal were a specific outcome—every child becomes an entrepreneur, every grandchild joins the family business, and so on—then you would drive yourself mad trying to control variables that refuse to be controlled. But if the goal is creating conditions where meaning can be discovered and built upon, you can succeed without knowing in advance what form that meaning will take. Christi built a winery. Her cousin started a backpacking gear company. Another relative became a doctor. The common thread isn't the career; it's the builder orientation that each brought to their work. It's the joyful struggle and the pursuit of self-actualization that matter most.

The Multiplication Effect

When the contagion takes hold—when multiple family members are building, transforming, and pursuing meaning in ways that reinforce each other—something remarkable happens. The network effects compound.

Each builder becomes a node that connects to external networks:

business relationships, professional communities, social circles, and extended family. When those nodes are interconnected through the family mesh, the family gains access to all those external networks. Opportunities flow in. Perspectives diversify. The adjacent possible expands. A family member building in one industry learns something relevant to a cousin building in another industry, and the insight transfers through the mesh. Value isn't just transmitted throughout the network—it's brought into the network and compounded.

This is the multiplication that connected families achieve across generations. The original wealth-creator built something from nothing. The next generation, if they become builders rather than beneficiaries, doesn't just preserve that legacy—they multiply it by adding their own ventures, networks, and transformations to the family's portfolio of capability. Human capital compounds faster than financial capital because each builder develops skills, relationships, and resilience that accrue to the family system. The mesh network becomes a petri dish for contagions to spread effectively.

Melissa Osborn's three hundred family members represent an extraordinary potential network. Most of them, by her account, are loosely connected at best—nodes that could be part of a mesh but currently float in relative isolation. Her work, perhaps like yours, is to build connective tissue, to tell stories, and to create visibility into what different branches are building to activate that latent network. She may not succeed with everyone; we all have our agency. But if even a fraction of those three hundred catch the contagion—if they start building, start connecting, and start creating their own first-generation stories—the multiplication effects could be extraordinary.

"How do we create new first generations?" she asked. The answer is: You create conditions for contagion, build the mesh network that allows transformation to spread, establish a culture of coaching that supports everyone's journey, and then trust the process. Some will catch it. They'll become the next Christi, the next builder whose visible transformation activates others.

Principles

1. **Purpose spreads through proximity.** Self-actualization is contagious, but the contagion requires closeness—the ability to observe transformation as it happens, in enough detail to be activated by it. Stories of ancestors who built things are valuable as anchoring context, but they lack the immediacy that sparks mimicry. What spreads contagion is a family member who is visibly building right now: struggling, iterating, transforming in real time. Families that want to transmit builder values should optimize for observable transformation, not just celebrated achievement.
2. **The most powerful family teaching method is modeled transformation.** Children learn more from watching their parents build than from hearing lectures about hard work. Siblings learn more from observing each other's struggles than from formal family education programs. The mesh network of a healthy family creates countless opportunities for this kind of observational learning, with each node potentially inspiring others through visible pursuit of meaning. The family's role is to build the network, make transformation legible across it, and then trust the mimicry dynamics that are hardwired into human nature.

Application Examples

These ideas matter most when translated from concept to concrete action. Below is a sampling of age-appropriate prompts to guide you with your children or grandchildren.

Get the full list at WealthTrapBook.com/list.

- **Ages 5–8**

  Let your children see you work. Not just the polished outputs, but the messy middle—the problem you're trying to solve, the frustration when something isn't working, the satisfaction when you figure it out. Allow them to tag along to meetings, site visits, or other situations where you're trying to make something happen.

- **Ages 9–12**

  Find a cousin or family friend who is building something and arrange a visit to expose your kids to how their business or project works. Ask them to share what they're struggling with and how they're working through it.

- **Ages 13–17**

  Make your own transformation visible and discussable. If you're working on something new—a project, a health goal, a learning challenge, and so on—share the process with your teenagers. Invite their questions. Be honest about struggles. This is counterintuitive, since teenagers often seem uninterested, but the modeling registers even when they don't show it. You're demonstrating that building is a lifelong pursuit.

- **Ages 18–25**

  Facilitate mesh network connections with other young builders in and outside the family. Introductions to relatives pursuing interesting paths. Invitations to gatherings where people share what they're working on. A builder's dinner where people come and discuss what they're creating and where they could use help. The goal is to surround your young adult with visible transformation, so that building becomes normal rather than exceptional. They will become what they have the opportunity to observe; make sure they're observing builders.

CHAPTER 12

A New Founding Moment

Within our lifetimes, it is possible—likely, even—that artificial intelligence and robotics will eliminate the need for most human labor. The trajectory is clear to anyone paying attention. Trucks will drive themselves. Legal documents will draft themselves. Medical diagnoses will generate themselves. Code will write itself. Many of the jobs that structured human life for centuries—the jobs that gave people reason to get up in the morning, skills to develop, colleagues to collaborate with, and identities to inhabit—will evaporate in ways that make the industrial revolution look like a minor disruption.

What happens to human beings when they are no longer needed as they once were?

Yuval Noah Harari offers one answer. Harari is an Israeli historian and philosopher who has become an influential public intellectual. His books have sold tens of millions of copies. He advises the World

Economic Forum and has been publicly praised by Bill Gates, Mark Zuckerberg, and Barack Obama. When the global elite gather to discuss the future, Harari is often found framing the conversation.

Here is what he says is coming:

> In the Industrial Revolution of the nineteenth century, what humanity basically learned to produce was all kinds of stuff, like textiles, shoes, weapons, and vehicles, and this was enough for the very few countries that underwent the revolution to subjugate everybody else. What we're talking about now is like a second Industrial Revolution, but the product this time will not be textiles, machines, vehicles, or even weapons. The product this time will be humans themselves.
>
> We're basically learning to produce bodies and minds. Bodies and minds are going to be the two main products of the next wave of all these changes. And if there is a gap between those that know how to produce bodies and minds and those that do not, then this is far greater than anything we saw before in history. And this time, if you're not fast enough to become part of the revolution, then you'll probably become extinct.[1]

"The biggest question maybe in economics and politics of the coming decades," he later added, "will be what to do with all these useless people." See where he's going? He continued: "The problem is more boredom, and what to do with them, and how will they find some sense of meaning in life when they are basically meaningless, worthless. My best guess at present is a combination of drugs and computer games."[2]

Read that again. One of the most celebrated thinkers of our era, advising the institutions that shape global policy, believes that the future holds vast populations of "useless" people whose best hope for contentment is pharmaceutical sedation and passive digital consumption. Not purpose. Not contribution. Not meaning. *Drugs and computer games.*

This is not Orwell. This is not the floating-chair dystopia of *WALL-E*, where humans rendered physically helpless and mentally disengaged by endless comfort drift through life as overgrown infants. Those were warnings, fictional cautionary tales meant to shock us into choosing differently. What Harari describes should be considered a plan. It is the stated expectation of people with significant influence over how our world is being designed. And the most chilling part is the casual acceptance—the shrug embedded in "my best guess"—as if the reduction of billions of human beings to sedated consumers is simply an engineering problem to be managed rather than a moral catastrophe to be prevented.

And here is the most terrifying part: He's not entirely wrong about the trajectory. There already exist large segments of our population who, consciously or unconsciously, have concluded that they are not capable of creating value for others. Their default is to extract value from systems rather than contribute to them. We see it in the expansion of social welfare. We see it in the loss of cultural identity within certain communities. We see it in the epidemic of anxiety, depression, and deaths of despair among people who have material comfort but no sense of purpose.

We are already sick. And we haven't even arrived at the future that Harari describes—the one that will fully enable this sickness to metastasize.

The real question is whether that future is inevitable.

The Prosperity Paradox at Scale

In the preface, we explained that this book would address a problem that afflicts affluent families: the prosperity paradox. Wealth removes necessity. Necessity once provided the friction that developed capability, character, and meaning. Without deliberate intervention, children raised in abundance drift toward consumption rather than creation, becoming beneficiaries rather than builders.

But, as you may recall, we also mentioned that the prosperity paradox is not just your problem. It is about to become *everyone's* problem.

The families reading this book are at the tip of the spear. You are experiencing at a nuclear level what society will soon experience broadly. When artificial intelligence and automation deliver increased abundance to the masses—when basic needs can be met with minimal to no human effort—the entire species will face the question that has kept you up at night: How do we find meaning when we don't have to work?

This reframes your responsibility entirely.

You are not just trying to raise good kids. You are not just trying to preserve family wealth across generations. *You are pioneering the adaptation that humanity will need to survive the age of abundance.* If affluent families cannot figure out how to escape the wealth trap—how to transmit purpose, agency, and the capacity for meaningful contribution to the next generation—what hope does broader society have when abundance arrives for everyone?

The stakes are civilizational. And here is the crucial insight: The two tasks before you—building a family culture that produces builders and investing in the civilizational infrastructure for a new founding—are not actually separate pursuits. They are nested. The family operating system you build is a prototype. The builders you raise become architects of societal renewal. The culture that solves the prosperity paradox in your household must eventually be transmitted to every household. Your family, and our families in the aggregate, become contributing elements to a broader renewal.

America at 250

This book is being published during the 250th anniversary of the United States of America—a milestone that invites reflection on where we've been and where we're headed.

The historical pattern is not encouraging. Civilizations tend to follow predictable arcs. They are founded by builders who sacrifice, struggle, and create institutions that enable flourishing. The next generation inherits those institutions and maintains them, perhaps adding incremental improvements. The generation after that begins to take the institutions for granted, consuming the benefits without understanding the costs that produced them. And then comes decline—a loss of shared purpose, a fracturing of social cohesion, and a turn toward decadence and extraction rather than creation and contribution.

Historians and social scientists have long observed that great powers rise and fall with eerie regularity. Sir John Glubb, a British military officer who spent decades studying the life cycles of civilizations, documented a pattern spanning three millennia: From the Assyrians to the Persians, from Rome to the Arab caliphates, from the Spanish Empire to the British, the average lifespan of a dominant power is approximately 250 years—roughly ten generations.[3]

More recently, Samuel Arbesman at Harvard examined forty-one empires across three thousand years and found a strikingly similar pattern: a mean imperial lifespan of approximately 220 years.[4] Despite vast differences in geography, technology, religion, and political structure, the consistency held. The Assyrians and the Spanish, the Romans and the Ottomans, the Mongols and the British—all rose and fell within a similar time frame.

The consistency is striking. Empires and large nation-states seem to follow a remarkably similar trajectory. They rise through courage, sacrifice, and collective effort. They consolidate through commerce and institutional development. They peak in affluence and cultural achievement. And then, gradually at first and then with gathering speed, they decline.

The prevailing pattern is not mechanical, nor is it fate. But the pattern is consistent enough to demand our attention. The question is whether there will be builders ready to meet that moment.

While working on this book, I was asked to present some of our ideas to a diverse gathering of wealthy individuals. After my remarks, I was asked what we do in a world where nobody needs to work. My answer: We build civilization.

But what does that actually mean? We cannot predict what a radically transformed economy and society will look like. The Founders in 1776 could not have imagined the internet. The industrialists of the early twentieth century could not have foreseen the rise of artificial intelligence. We stand at a similar threshold, peering into a future that will differ from our present in ways we cannot yet comprehend.

What we do know is this: If we build builders, they will figure it out. This is why the internal work of family culture and the external work of civilizational building are ultimately one and the same. You cannot contribute to the infrastructure of the future without first developing builders capable of constructing it.

Children who understand value creation—who have internalized that a successful life lies in being of service to others—will identify and solve problems regardless of how the economy restructures. Young adults who have pursued meaning and discovered what makes them come alive will not be paralyzed when old career paths disappear. People who have built rich networks of relationships will have access to opportunities and support that isolated individuals cannot imagine. Those who are adaptive, resilient, and antifragile will not merely survive disruption; they will thrive in it.

We cannot give our children a map to a territory that doesn't yet exist. But we can give them the capabilities that make them skilled navigators of any terrain. The operating systems we build in our families—the values we transmit, the experiences we design, the orientations we model—determine whether our children will be equipped to respond to whatever demands and opportunities emerge in a world we can scarcely fathom from where we now stand.

This is our new founding moment. Not a repetition of 1776, but a parallel challenge: to build the human, cultural, and institutional infrastructure that will allow civilization to flourish in an age of unprecedented abundance. The Founders built a political architecture to protect liberty from tyranny. We must build a human architecture to protect meaning from abundance. That architecture begins in your family, but it cannot end there. The systems you develop, if they work, become the blueprints that other families will need.

The Arc of Stewardship

We have spent this book discussing how to form the next generation. But before we can transmit something, we must possess it ourselves. The frameworks and practices we've outlined are not just tools for raising children—they are mirrors that reflect our own orientation toward the resources, opportunities, and responsibilities we've obtained.

Every person exists somewhere along an arc from extraction to creation (see figure 24). The position we occupy determines not only our own flourishing, but what we are capable of transmitting to those who come after us.

Extraction is the beneficiary stage, where all children begin. A person at this level (whether a child or an adult) operates with a "what's in it for me?" approach. A beneficiary extracts value created by others and relies on inherited systems and comfort. The person at this stage is fragile—a consumer of meaning rather than a contributor. They may have resources, but they have no resilience. When circumstances change, they crumble.

THE ARC OF STEWARDSHIP

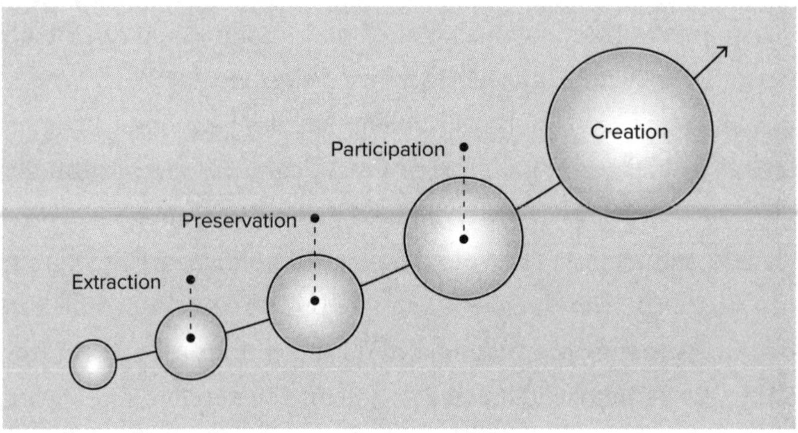

Figure 24

We have been clear throughout this book that this is the stage we want to help your children avoid. But we need to be equally clear: Many parents find themselves in this stage without recognizing it. If your primary orientation toward your family's wealth is "What can I get from it?"—even if what you're getting is security, status, or freedom from work you don't enjoy—you may be modeling extraction for your children. They will learn from what you do, not what you say.

Preservation is the stewardship stage. A person operating at this level considers how they should protect financial assets. They guard assets, traditions, and reputation—but often mistake maintenance for mission. The person at this stage achieves stability, but stability without renewal. They orbit the past rather than build the future.

This is where many affluent families get stuck. Preservation feels responsible. For inheritors, it feels like doing what the wealth creator would have wanted—and it feels fair to future generations, so they can be beneficiaries too. But preservation alone is a slow death. Systems that are only maintained, never renewed, eventually become irrelevant or collapse. The family that focuses exclusively on protecting what was built will watch that inheritance lose meaning and potency over time—not because the assets disappear (though they often do), but because the purpose that animated their creation has been forgotten.

Participation is the apprentice stage. A person operating here thinks about how they can contribute to others. Their behavior is engagement with purpose, taking small risks, and developing capability through experiments rather than entitlement. They build confidence and competence. Meaning becomes personal rather than inherited.

This is what the experiments and feedback loops we discussed earlier are designed to produce. The child who runs a lemonade stand, the teenager who starts a small venture, the young adult who takes on a challenging role—they are all at the participation stage, learning through doing that they can create value in the world. But again: This stage is not just for children. Adults who have coasted on inherited wealth or established success need participation too. They need to put themselves in positions where they are learning, struggling, and contributing—not just managing and consuming.

Creation is the builder stage. Rather than wondering what's in it for us, we think about what's in it for others. We wonder what we can build that will outlast us. The behavior is deploying capital—human, financial, and philanthropic—to create new value in alignment with purpose. The person at this stage generates renewal and regeneration. They are antifragile because they are always building, always adapting, always creating new sources of meaning and value.

This is the destination. This is why builders exist and how they operate. In this book, we've been discussing how to raise such builders. But raising builders requires becoming one yourself. Not in the past tense—something you did before you had resources. In the present tense. Now. Continuously.

The arc of stewardship is not a ladder you climb once. It is a daily choice about how you will orient toward your resources, your time, and your life.

You Are the Child

You thought this book was about your children. It is. Everything we've discussed—meaning, stories, shared language, operating systems, joyful struggle, and much more—all of it is designed to help you raise builders rather than beneficiaries.

But this chapter is about you.

Together, we are entering an entirely new world. The pace of change is so dramatic, and the disruption so profound, that the mental models and life patterns that served you well are becoming obsolete. The career paths you followed will likely not be available to your children. The institutions you trusted may transform beyond recognition. The assumptions about how life works that you absorbed growing up are being invalidated in real time.

In this sense, you are the child. You are the one who needs to develop new capabilities, new frameworks, and new ways of understanding how to create value in a world that looks nothing like the one you were once prepared for.

This requires psychological flexibility that does not come naturally. If you cannot articulate your own directionality of purpose—if you cannot answer, in terms of meaning and contribution, the question of who you are becoming—you will be lost. Purpose is your compass.

Without it, you will drift just as surely as any trust fund kid who never had to work.

The families who solve this problem will have something to teach all of us. And that is why your responsibility extends beyond your own household.

The Multigenerational Mindset

What we are calling you to is not a project that can be completed in a generation.

THE MULTIGENERATIONAL MINDSET

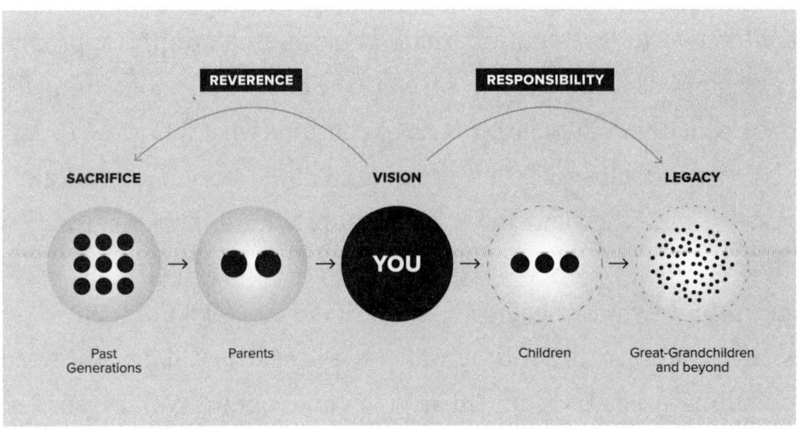

Figure 25

Consider where you stand in the flow of time. Behind you are past generations—ancestors who sacrificed, built, struggled, and created the conditions that made your life possible. Some of them you knew. Most of them you didn't. But their choices compound forward through time, shaping possibilities they never could have imagined.

Your parents stand closer, their influence more direct. The values they transmitted, the systems they created, the examples they set—these formed you in ways you're still discovering.

And now here you are. The product of all that came before, and the source of all that comes after.

Ahead of you are your children's lives, which you will directly shape through your choices, your presence, and your modeling. And beyond them, fading into the future as ripples from a stone dropped in water, are grandchildren, great-grandchildren, and countless descendants you will never meet but whose lives you are already influencing.

This is the multigenerational mindset (see figure 25): the recognition that you are not an isolated individual but a link in a chain that stretches backward and forward through time. Looking backward, the appropriate response is reverence—honoring the sacrifice that built the world that you inherited. Looking forward, the appropriate response is responsibility—feeling the duty to add something for future generations, not just protect or consume what was given to you.

Most people live as if they are the end of the story. They consume what was built for them and leave nothing behind. This is extraction extended across time—taking from the past without giving to the future.

The builder mindset is different. Builders understand themselves as characters in the middle of a very long story. They received something precious from those who came before (values, stories, resources, relationships, hard-won wisdom, and sacrifices made on their behalf). They intend to leave something more precious for those who come after. The meaning of their lives is inseparable from this continuity.

This is what it means to build for descendants you'll never meet. It means making choices today that will compound across generations. It means investing in institutions, values, systems, and human capital that will outlast your own lifespan. It means accepting responsibility not only for your children, but for the unborn descendants of your children's children.

The Engine of Human Progress

Earlier in this book, we introduced the engine of human progress—the integration of financial capital, philanthropic capital, and human capital into a unified system that compounds across generations. We placed that engine within the context of the family operating system, showing how these three forms of capital can work together rather than at cross purposes.

Now we need to revisit that engine in light of everything we've discussed.

The engine exists in some form. Every family with resources has the components—financial capital generating returns, some portion flowing to philanthropy, and human capital developing (or failing to develop) in the next generation. But for most families, these components are loosely stitched together rather than integrated into a unified system. The fuel lines leak. The timing is off. The parts work against each other as often as they might work together. What could be a powerful engine capable of compounding impact across generations instead sputters along, consuming resources without producing the forward momentum that a well-functioning engine can produce.

The new founding moment requires powerful engines that produce this momentum. Not just in your family, but across thousands of families. Not just for one generation, but for generations to come. The infrastructure of civilization is built by people who take seriously their responsibility to leave things better than they found them—and who have the resources, the capability, and the orientation to actually do it.

This is where your responsibility expands beyond your own household. But notice: This expansion is not a pivot away from your family but one that flows directly from it. The builders you raise are the human capital available for civilizational work. The operating system you develop is the intellectual capital that can be shared. The proof that your family flourishes in abundance is the contagion that makes others believe it's possible and inspires their own self-actualization. Your family's internal success is the prerequisite for external contribution—and your external contribution is what gives your family's work meaning beyond itself.

We believe the question is urgent. The window for building the infrastructure that will allow civilization to flourish in the age of abundance is not infinite. The forces pulling toward the Harari future—drugs and computer games for the useless masses—are powerful and accelerating. Every family that figures out how to transmit builder values is a data point proving that another path is possible. Every family that fails becomes evidence for the cynics who believe that humans in this era will be, as Harari said, "basically meaningless, worthless."

Freedom Through Responsibility

We began this chapter with a dark vision of the future—one in which abundance leads not to flourishing but to meaninglessness. Of course, this future is not inevitable, but avoiding it requires intentional work by people on the front line who understand what's at stake and have the resources to fight back.

The core insight is rather simple: Freedom without responsibility dissolves into decadence. This is true for individuals, families, and civilizations.

The affluent child who is given freedom without responsibility does not flourish. They drift. They consume. They become anxious and depressed despite having every material advantage. This pattern repeats across countless families, and we have shown you throughout this book the systems and practices that can interrupt it.

But the same principle applies at larger scales. A society that pursues freedom without responsibility will follow the same trajectory—drift, consumption, anxiety, and collapse. The political freedom won by the Founders requires responsible citizens to sustain it. The economic freedom generated by markets requires responsible participants to maintain it. The personal freedom made possible by abundance requires responsible individuals to make it meaningful.

This is why we say that true autonomy emerges when wealth is viewed as fuel for contribution rather than permission to drift. The child who understands their resources as fuel for building—not as an excuse for idleness—will use their freedom to create rather than consume. They will seek out challenges rather than avoiding them. They will take responsibility for outcomes rather than expecting others to solve their problems.

And the same is true for you.

Your wealth is not the end of your journey. Consider it, rather, as fuel for the work that remains. That work is partly within your family—raising the next generation to be builders, not beneficiaries. But it is also beyond your family—contributing to the infrastructure of civilization that will determine whether the age of abundance becomes a golden age or a dark one. The meaning architecture you build—the systems and practices that help your family flourish in abundance—has value far beyond your household. You are solving the prosperity paradox before it becomes everyone's problem. What works for your family today becomes the model that civilization will need tomorrow.

The Call

You have read this book because something in you knows that the conventional path is not working. The wealth you've built or inherited is not automatically producing the outcomes you want for your children. The society around you is not trending in directions that give you confidence about the future. You sense that something different is required, but you haven't been sure what.

Here is what we are asking of you:

First, examine where you stand on the arc of stewardship. Not where you think you stand, and not where you stood in the past—where you actually stand today. Are you extracting, preserving, participating, or creating? Be honest. Your children will learn from what you do, and they will see through any pretense.

Second, commit to your own ongoing transformation. You are not finished. The world is changing too fast for anyone to rest on past accomplishments. We must have childlike curiosity and resilience in a rapidly changing society. Find your own experiments to run, your own skills to develop, your own contributions to make. Model for your children what it looks like to be a lifelong builder.

Third, be the builder by implementing the systems and practices we've described throughout this book. The family operating system. The designed environments for joyful struggle. The experiments with feedback loops. The shared language and shared meaning. The contagion of self-actualization. Don't let these linger on the pages of this book as mere abstract ideas. They are specific practices that produce specific outcomes. Do them.

Fourth, expand your vision beyond your own family. The new founding moment needs more than individual families getting their houses in order. It needs coordinated investment in the institutions, programs, and infrastructure that will form builders at scale. It needs philanthropic capital directed toward human capital development. It needs people who understand what's at stake to work together on solutions. And it needs families who recognize that the culture they build at home is the seed of everything else. (In Appendix B, we're including a Constitution for a New Founding, as a template your family might consider.)

But the most important resource is not any particular tool or program. The most important one is the shift in orientation that we hope this book has catalyzed.

You are not just a wealthy person trying to avoid spoiling your kids. You are a pioneer on the frontier of human flourishing, facing a challenge that all of humanity will eventually face. Your success or failure matters not only to your family but to our entire species. Build the solution so it can be distributed to others.

The wealth trap is real, but it is not a death sentence. Families can transmit builder values across generations. Children can be raised with meaning and purpose even in the absence of material necessity. Human beings can flourish in abundance if—and only if—they are formed with the capability and orientation to contribute rather than consume.

This is the new founding moment. The Founders of 1776 pledged their lives, their fortunes, and their sacred honor to the cause of liberty. We are asking you to pledge your resources, your attention, and your sustained effort to the cause of *meaning*—to building the human architecture that will allow your descendants, and all descendants, to live lives of purpose in the age of abundance.

The alternative is drugs and computer games.

The choice is yours.

Principles

1. **Freedom without responsibility dissolves into decadence.** This is true for individuals, families, and civilizations. The affluent child given freedom without responsibility drifts toward consumption and meaninglessness. The society that pursues freedom without responsibility follows the same trajectory. The antidote is not less freedom but more responsibility, ensuring

that every expansion of possibility comes with a corresponding expansion of accountability. Families that understand this raise children who see their resources not as permission to drift but as fuel for building.

2. **True autonomy emerges when wealth is viewed as fuel for contribution.** The person who understands their resources as fuel for meaningful work—rather than as an end in themselves—will use freedom to create rather than consume. They will seek challenges rather than avoiding them. They will take responsibility for outcomes rather than expecting rescue. This orientation must be modeled before it can be transmitted. Parents who demonstrate that wealth enables contribution, not retirement from contribution, raise children who carry the same understanding into adulthood.

Application: Your Checklist

Unlike previous chapters, this is a list for you, the parent or grandparent. Here we offer just a sampling of the broader checklist and self-assessment you can find at WealthTrapBook.com/list.

Self-Assessment

- ☐ I can honestly identify where I currently stand on the arc of stewardship (extraction, preservation, participation, or creation).
- ☐ I have a clear articulation of my own directionality of purpose—who I am becoming, not just who I have been.
- ☐ I am actively running experiments in my own life, not just managing and consuming.

- [ ] I am modeling builder behavior that my children can observe and mimic.
- [ ] I can explain to my children why our family has resources and what responsibility comes with them.

Family Systems

- [ ] We have implemented a family operating system with regular rhythms of communication and accountability.
- [ ] We have created environments where our children experience joyful struggle—difficulty connected to meaning.
- [ ] We have structured experiments with feedback loops that allow our children to build evidence portfolios.
- [ ] We have developed shared language that reinforces builder values and makes our family's purpose concrete.
- [ ] We have built a mesh network of relationships that allows self-actualization to spread contagiously.

Extended Responsibility

- [ ] I understand that my family's success or failure in transmitting builder values has implications beyond our household.
- [ ] I have considered how our philanthropic capital could be directed toward human capital development at scale.
- [ ] I am connected with other families working on similar challenges, sharing what works and learning from others.
- [ ] I have a multigenerational vision that extends beyond my children to descendants I will never meet.
- [ ] I am prepared to invest sustained effort—not just money—in the infrastructure of the new founding moment.

Immediate Actions

- ☐ Have a conversation with your spouse about where your family stands on the frameworks in this book.
- ☐ Identify one experiment you will run in your own life in the next thirty days to model builder behavior.
- ☐ Review your family's current systems (financial, philanthropic, governance) through the lens of human capital development.
- ☐ Begin drafting a family constitution that articulates your purpose and the responsibilities that come with your resources.
- ☐ Reach out to at least one other family navigating similar challenges to build your network of mutual support.

Conclusion

You picked up this book because something was bothering you.

Maybe it was a specific moment: a child who seemed unmoored despite every advantage, a grandchild who couldn't articulate what they wanted from life, or a family meeting where the next generation seemed more interested in consumption than contribution. Or, more likely, the issue was more vague—a quiet dread that the wealth you've built or inherited might be doing something to your family that you can't quite name but can definitely feel.

That worry is wisdom, not weakness. The families who destroy themselves across generations are rarely the ones who saw the danger coming; they're the ones who assumed that financial capital was the metric of success. You're reading this because you refused to make that assumption. You sensed that prosperity without purpose leads somewhere dark, and you went looking for a different path.

Now you have one.

You understand that money is stored energy waiting to be directed, and that it amplifies whatever character and culture it flows through. You know that comfort, left unexamined, corrodes capability—and that institutions, however helpful, cannot raise your children for you. You've seen how meaning emerges at the intersection of building, feedback, and contribution, and why a life without that intersection drifts toward emptiness, no matter how full the accounts.

You have frameworks: the family operating system, the meaning profile, the experiments with feedback loops, the mesh network, the arc of stewardship, and many more. You have principles: that struggle can be joyful when connected to meaning, that human capital compounds faster than financial capital, that the most powerful teaching method is modeled transformation, and that freedom without responsibility dissolves into decadence.

What you don't have is a guarantee.

No framework or idea can promise that every child will become a builder. Human beings have agency. They make choices. Some will catch the contagion of self-actualization; others will choose drift despite every intervention. But the odds change dramatically based on what you do. Families who implement these practices will produce builders at far higher rates than families who simply hope for the best or assume that things will work out. The work we've described is not guaranteed to succeed, but failing to do it is almost guaranteed to fail.

The work itself is not glamorous. There will be no dramatic moment when everything clicks into place. Instead, there will be thousands of ordinary moments (with some peak moments interspersed!): a dinner conversation where your teenager discloses the purpose they're envisioning, an experiment that fails but teaches something irreplaceable, or a child who struggles through something hard and emerges knowing they can handle difficulty. These moments are the building blocks of human capital, laid one on top of another until something sturdy emerges.

Here is something important to remember: Raising builders is less about *what* your children accomplish than *who* they become. The lemonade stand, the first venture, the failed experiment, the service project—none of these necessarily matter in themselves. They are vehicles through which your children *build themselves*. You are not trying to produce impressive outcomes you can brag about at dinner parties. You are developing their capacity and character. The stuff they build is just the gymnasium where that development happens.

Your job is to keep showing up. To resist the temptation to outsource the hard parts to institutions that don't share your stakes. To hold the tension between giving your children enough comfort to thrive and enough struggle to grow. To model, in your own life, the pursuit of meaning over ease—so that when they look at you, they see someone still building, still learning, still becoming.

And that work extends beyond your own household.

Affluent families are at the tip of the spear—experiencing now what society will soon face broadly. The prosperity paradox is coming for everyone as automation delivers abundance to populations unprepared to handle the drift of lost necessity. The vision of "useless" people sedated by drugs and entertainment is not inevitable, but it is the default trajectory if no one demonstrates a better way.

Every family that escapes the wealth trap becomes a proof point. Every builder raised is evidence that meaning can survive abundance. Your success matters not only to the people around your dinner table, but to a civilization that desperately needs examples of what flourishing in abundance looks like.

So here is where we leave you: not with certainty, but with a charge.

Look around your dinner table. Those faces—those specific, irreplaceable people you love—are who this is for. The child who frustrates you. The teenager who seems allergic to effort. The young adult who hasn't found their footing. They are why you read this book. They are why the work matters.

The energy you've stored must flow somewhere. It will either fuel building or subsidize drift. It will either develop capability or cushion comfort. It will either compound into human capital that outlasts you or dissipate into consumption that leaves nothing behind.

You now know enough to make that choice wisely. You have the frameworks. You have the principles. What remains is the work itself: patient, unglamorous, and essential. The work of building builders. The work of transmitting not just resources but resourcefulness. The work of raising human beings who understand that wealth is fuel for contribution, not permission to coast.

That work begins—or continues—the moment you set down this book.

Ready to build?

Appendix A: How We Can Help

The vision we've cast in this book is ambitious. Building a family culture that produces builders, solving the prosperity paradox, and contributing to the infrastructure of a new founding moment—these are not small undertakings. If you're feeling the weight of that call and wondering where to begin, you're certainly not alone. Many families find that having a guide makes the difference between intention and implementation.

We've spent years developing resources and services to help families like yours put these ideas into practice. Below are two paths, depending on where you are and what kind of support would be most valuable.

NextGen Builders

I operate NextGen Builders, a program designed to help affluent families raise children and young adults with the builder mindset from an early age. The program offers two core components:

First, an online academy filled with educational content that empowers parents to teach their children the ideas at the heart of this book—meaning and value creation, along with financial concepts, entrepreneurial mindset, and more. These are videos and supplementary resources that parents can use directly with their kids, turning many of the ideas we've discussed into practical family learning. The academy offers a structured path through concepts that can otherwise feel overwhelming, with age-appropriate content that meets your children where they are and grows with them over time.

Second, family consulting and coaching for UHNW families who want direct support. My team and I work with parents and grandparents to help them implement these ideas within their specific family systems—addressing particular challenges, designing experiments, and building the operating rhythms that sustain a family culture of builders. This is personalized, direct support for someone seeking guidance and accountability. Every family is different: the dynamics, the ages, the history, the obstacles. What works for one family may not work for yours. The consulting relationship allows us to assess your specific situation, identify gaps, and build a plan that actually fits your life—not a generic framework, but a tailored human capital approach that addresses the real challenges you're facing with your children or grandchildren right now.

NextGen Builders is part of Libertas Network (see Libertas.org), a nonprofit organization I lead that helps families learn and apply the ideas of human flourishing. Through this broader ecosystem I have helped millions of children learn these ideas through the *Tuttle Twins* books, launch real businesses through the Kids Markets program, and develop the critical thinking and civic engagement that builders require. If you have younger children or grandchildren and would like educational resources or direct consulting support, visit NextGenBuilders.com.

Belief Partners

Taylor operates Belief Partners, a human-capital and trust-architecture advisory built for enterprising families who want their wealth to produce builders, not just beneficiaries. Belief Partners helps families design the structures, governance, and operating rhythms that make multigenerational flourishing repeatable. This work often includes: shaping (or reshaping) family office capabilities; aligning estate plans and trust distribution logic with the development of capability; establishing governance that matches your family's purpose; and building a practical family operating system that integrates financial capital, philanthropic capital, and human capital into one coherent engine. Taylor's work focuses on three pillars: architecture (trusts and incentives), governance (roles and decision-making), and development (coaching and capability-building). This is for families who sense that their current system funds comfort well, but doesn't reliably produce capability, cohesion, or contribution.

Alongside system design, Taylor also works directly with beneficiaries, grantors, trustees, and family office leaders through coaching and education—helping individuals navigate the relational and psychological complexity of wealth while building real agency, contribution, and stewardship over time.

Whether your family is modernizing an existing system or building one for the first time, Belief Partners brings a design-oriented approach grounded in lived family-office experience to reduce entropy, increase alignment, and build the conditions for initiative to compound across generations. If you're looking for help with the architecture—not just advice—visit Belief.Partners.

Operating in parallel, the Belief Institute is a nonprofit research-and-action lab focused on the prosperity paradox: In a world where material constraints are falling, meaning and agency don't automatically rise. The Institute treats this not as a moral failing or a political debate, but as an infrastructure problem—a design challenge that can be studied, tested, and improved. Its purpose is to develop and validate meaning systems: the practical architectures that help individuals, families, and institutions sustain agency, dignity, and purpose within conditions of enduring abundance. The Institute publishes research, builds open-source frameworks, convenes practitioners, and pilots interventions—so the next era of prosperity produces not just comfort, but builders, citizens, and contributors.

Wherever you are in your journey, the most important step is the next one. We wrote this book to change how families think about wealth, meaning, and legacy. We built these programs to help families act on that thinking. If either path resonates, reach out. The work of building builders is too important to do alone.

Appendix B: A Constitution for a New Founding

Preamble

We stand at a threshold unlike any in human history.

For millennia, scarcity shaped human life. The need to survive forced people to build, to struggle, to create value for one another. That necessity, however harsh, forged character. It gave structure to days and meaning to effort. It bound generations together in a shared project of survival and progress.

Now, for many, abundance is becoming the norm rather than the exception. Technology and accumulated wealth are removing the external pressures that once demanded growth. This is, in one sense, a triumph—the fulfillment of humanity's long struggle against need. But it is also a crisis. When necessity disappears, so does the scaffolding that shaped human development. Comfort replaces contribution. Consumption replaces creation. Drift replaces purpose. This is the wealth trap.

Some share a cynical outlook on humanity's future in an age of abundance—an elitist perspective that sees most people as worthless and meaningless, fit only for sedation and passive entertainment. We reject this vision entirely. We refuse to accept that human beings are problems to be managed rather than potential to be cultivated. We believe that every person is capable of creating value, of pursuing meaning, of contributing to something greater than themselves.

Therefore, as families committed to human flourishing across generations, we do hereby adopt this Constitution for a New Founding—a summary of the beliefs we hold, the commitments we make, and the civilization we intend to build.

Article I: Truths We Hold

We affirm these truths as the foundation upon which we build:

On Human Nature. Human beings are made to create. We are not passive consumers meant to be adrift in our own lives, but active agents capable of shaping the world. When we build, struggle, and contribute, we come alive. When we drift, consume, and extract, we wither.

On Wealth. True wealth is the capacity to create value for others. Financial capital is the by-product of human capital, never the reverse. Families who forget this nourish the symptoms of success while starving its sources.

On Meaning. Meaning cannot be inherited, purchased, or bestowed. It emerges when a person builds something they care about, receives honest feedback from the world, and knows their effort served others. Without this intersection, no amount of comfort can prevent the quiet corrosion of purposelessness.

On Struggle. Struggle is the prerequisite of flourishing. The question is not whether our children will struggle, but whether their struggle will be connected to meaning. Joyful struggle—difficulty in pursuit of something that matters—builds the character that comfort alone cannot produce.

On Freedom and Responsibility. Freedom without responsibility dissolves into decadence. The purpose of wealth is not to insulate our children from consequence but to expand their capacity for contribution. True autonomy emerges when resources are understood as fuel for creation, not permission to drift.

On Generations. We are links in a chain stretching backward and forward through time. Society is a partnership between the dead, the living, and the yet unborn. We inherit obligations from those who sacrificed before us; we hold duties to descendants we will never meet. This multigenerational mindset is a source of meaning—connecting our small lives to something vast and enduring.

Article II: Commitments to Our Family

In light of these truths, we commit to building a family of builders, not beneficiaries:

We will cultivate human capital rather than protect financial capital. The character, capability, and creativity of our family members matter more than the preservation of assets. We will invest in developing people with the same intentionality we bring to creating wealth.

We will design environments for joyful struggle. We will not shield our children from all difficulty, nor will we manufacture misery. We will create conditions where meaningful challenges are available, where effort connects to outcome, and where growth is possible through experience rather than instruction alone.

We will build systems, not just hopes. Love is not enough. Good intentions are not enough. We will construct a family operating system—rhythms of communication, shared language, rituals of connection, and structures of accountability—that transmits our values across generations.

We will model transformation, not just teach principles. Our children will learn more from watching us build than from hearing us lecture.

We commit to remaining builders ourselves so that self-actualization becomes contagious rather than theoretical.

We will raise creators, not consumers. We will measure success not by what our children accumulate but by what they contribute. We will celebrate the building of capability over the acquisition of credentials, the creation of value over the consumption of privilege.

We will think in generations. Our decisions will be informed not merely by what benefits our children, but by what strengthens our grandchildren's grandchildren. We create a better present for ourselves by envisioning and working to build an exciting future for generations yet unborn.

Article III: Commitments to Our Resources

Understanding that financial capital is stored energy awaiting direction, we commit to deploying our resources in service of creation:

We will use wealth as fuel, not as insulation. Our resources exist to expand what our family can build, learn, and contribute—not to buffer our children from every discomfort or consequence. We will resist the temptation to solve with money what should be solved with growth.

We will invest in capability, not just comfort. We will fund experiments, apprenticeships, ventures, and experiences that build human capital. We will measure the return on these investments not merely in financial terms but in the development of judgment, resilience, and the capacity to create value.

We will pursue meaningful consumption. We will not apologize for enjoying the fruits of our labor, but we will ensure that our consumption creates memory, connection, and growth rather than mere pleasure. We will ask of every significant expenditure: Does this strengthen who we are becoming?

We will reject hoarding as false prudence. Capital that sits idle, accumulating without purpose, is energy wasted. We will maintain appropriate reserves for resilience and opportunity, but we will not mistake fear for wisdom. Stored energy must eventually flow, or it loses its capacity to do good.

We will give to build, not merely to relieve. Our philanthropy will address not only immediate needs but long-term civilizational challenges. We will invest in the infrastructure of human flourishing—the institutions, frameworks, and ideas that will equip generations yet unborn to find meaning in a world transformed by abundance. We measure philanthropic success not by dollars deployed but by capacity built.

Article IV: Commitments to Society

Recognizing that strong families are the foundation of strong societies, we commit to building beyond our own household:

We will raise citizens, not just heirs. Our children will understand that they are inheritors not only of family wealth but of a civilization built by countless generations of sacrifice and effort. They will be equipped to contribute to the common good, to build institutions, and to strengthen the communities in which they live.

We will build institutions that outlast us. We will invest in the mediating structures of civil society—the organizations and communities that form human beings and transmit culture. We will not merely consume the benefits of these institutions but actively strengthen them for those who come after.

We will pioneer flourishing in abundance. We recognize that affluent families are experiencing now what broader society will soon face—the challenge of finding meaning when necessity no longer compels it. We accept the responsibility to solve this equation, to develop the models and practices that will help humanity thrive in an age of unprecedented plenty.

We will prove the cynics wrong. Against those who see the future as masses of purposeless people numbed by entertainment, we will demonstrate that human beings can flourish without external compulsion—that meaning can be cultivated, that builders can be raised, that creation is possible in any circumstance. Every family that gets this right becomes a proof point for civilization.

Article V: The Charge

This Constitution is not a document to be filed and forgotten. It is a declaration of who we are becoming and what we are building together.

We acknowledge that we will fall short. We will be tempted to drift toward comfort. We will make mistakes. We will sometimes forget what we have declared here. But we commit to returning, again and again, to these principles—to reading them aloud, to measuring ourselves against them, and to holding one another accountable to the vision we share.

We are not merely preserving wealth. We are building human capital—the skills, character, relationships, and wisdom that compound across generations. We are not merely raising children. We are participating in the construction of culture and systems that will empower multiple generations of builders.

We are not merely building a family. We are founding something that can endure—a lineage of creators, a culture of contribution, a living demonstration that abundance need not corrupt but can elevate.

This is our new founding moment. The prosperity paradox is real, but it is not a death sentence. The shirtsleeves-to-shirtsleeves cycle is common, but can be transcended. The future is not written. It will be built by those who choose to.

We so choose.

This Constitution for a New Founding is offered as a starting point for families committed to raising builders in an age of abundance. We encourage you to visit WealthTrapBook.com/constitution *to download this text, discuss it with your family, adapt it to your circumstances, and make it your own. Focus less on a rigid adherence to these specific words, and more on development of shared language and a shared commitment to what you are building together and why it matters. Gather your family and read what you come up with aloud. Discuss what resonates and what changes you wish to make. Then sign your names to whatever version emerges, and let it become a living document that orients your family's directionality of purpose for generations to come.*

Notes

Preface

1. "The Gilded Age and Beyond: The Persistence of Elite Wealth in American History," National Bureau of Economic Research, January 2025, https://www.nber.org/papers/w33355.
2. "Global Flourishing Study," Harvard Institute for Qualitative Social Science, accessed November 19, 2025, https://hfh.fas.harvard.edu/global-flourishing-study.
3. "The Happiest Country in the World Isn't What You Think," *New York Times*, April 30, 2025, https://www.nytimes.com/2025/04/30/opinion/happiness-economic-development.html.

Introduction

1. "The Most Important Graph in the World," Human Progress, December 13, 2016, https://humanprogress.org/the-most-important-graph-in-the-world/.
2. Edward Gibbon, *The History of the Decline and Fall of the Roman Empire* (M.F. Guizot, 1840), 529.
3. There were, of course, other factors—an overextended empire, devalued currency, civil war, increasing bureaucracy, and more. We contend, however, that a purposeful people pursuing their self-actualization can weather these and other storms, but that when vision and energy are lost, these and other problems become insurmountable and lead to collapse.
4. As quoted in Viktor E. Frankl, *Man's Search for Meaning* (Pocket Books, 1985), 126.
5. Dan Sullivan and Benjamin Hardy, *Who Not How: The Formula to Achieve Bigger Goals Through Accelerating Teamwork* (Hay House, 2020), 16.
6. "Quote Origin: Everybody Has Plans Until They Get Hit for the First

Time," Quote Investigator, August 25, 2021, https://quoteinvestigator.com/2021/08/25/plans-hit/.

7. Charles Francis Adams, ed., *Familiar Letters of John Adams and His Wife Abigail Adams During the Revolution* (Hurd and Houghton, 1876), 28.

Chapter 1

1. Claiborne Haw, interview with authors, November 26, 2025.
2. Claiborne was referencing (and experiencing) Proverbs 29:18, which reads: "Where there is no vision, the people perish."
3. Maslow did not originally teach his hierarchy of needs as a pyramid. The now-familiar pyramid diagram was added later by others to visualize his hierarchy more simply. He described a hierarchy of human needs, but he presented them as stages or classes of needs rather than as a geometric shape. In his writing he emphasized that people can pursue multiple needs at once and move back and forth among them, which does not fit the rigid "one level at a time" implication of the pyramid graphic.

Chapter 2

1. "The $400m Reclusive Heiress, Her Nurse and a Battle of Wills," *The Telegraph*, September 7, 2013, https://www.telegraph.co.uk/news/worldnews/northamerica/usa/10293694/The-400m-reclusive-heiress-her-nurse-and-a-battle-of-wills.html.
2. "The Peculiar Life of Huguette Clark," *DuJour*, accessed December 8, 2025, https://dujour.com/culture/huguette-clark-peculiar-life-trial/.
3. "'The Dust of Many a Hard-Fought Field' - Place Attachment and Agriculture at Minute Man," National Park Service, accessed December 9, 2025, https://www.nps.gov/articles/000/-the-dust-of-many-a-hard-fought-field-place-attachment-and-agriculture-at-minute-man.htm.

Chapter 3

1. "Powerball Winner Says He's Cursed," *ABC News*, April 5, 2007, https://abcnews.go.com/2020/powerball-winner-cursed/story?id=3012631.
2. "Doge, AI, Mars, and the Future of Humanity," *Katie Miller Podcast*, December 10, 2025, https://www.youtube.com/watch?v=bz5Hjk40FD4.

Chapter 4

1. Viktor E. Frankl, *Man's Search for Meaning* (Pocket Books, 1985), 95.
2. Frankl, *Man's Search for Meaning*, 126.
3. "King Vidor: A Pioneer of American Cinema," Texas State Historical Association, August 1, 1995, https://www.tshaonline.org/handbook/entries/vidor-king-wallis.
4. Frankl, *Man's Search for Meaning*, 17.
5. Frankl, *Man's Search for Meaning*, 133.
6. "Thomas Sowell: There Are No Solutions, Only Trade-offs," YouTube, accessed January 6, 2025, https://www.youtube.com/watch?v=3_EtIWmja-4; Sowell wrote in detail about this topic in his book *A Conflict of Visions: Ideological Origins of Political Struggles* (Basic Books, 2002).

Chapter 5

1. Kate Gardner, interview with authors, November 15, 2025.
2. Tamara Deutscher, ed., *Voices of Czechoslovak Socialists* (Committee to Defend Czechoslovak Socialists, 1977), 112.
3. Thomas Babington Macaulay, *The History of England from the Accession of James II*, vol. 2 (John B. Alden, 1883), 836.
4. Malachi 4:6.

Chapter 6

1. Edmund Burke, *Reflections on the Revolution in France* (John Sharpe, 1819), 135.
2. "The Stories That Bind Us," *New York Times*, March 15, 2013, https://www.nytimes.com/2013/03/17/fashion/the-family-stories-that-bind-us-this-life.html.
3. Thomas Powell, interview with authors, November 20, 2025.

Chapter 7

1. "The Gucci Wife and the Hitman: Fashion's Darkest Tale," *The Guardian*, July 24, 2016, https://www.theguardian.com/fashion/2016/jul/24/the-gucci-wife-and-the-hitman-fashions-darkest-tale.

2. "Inside U-Haul's Rollercoaster Ride from Nastiest Family Feud to Market Dominance," *Forbes*, February 10, 2016, https://www.forbes.com/sites/luisakroll/2016/02/10/inside-u-hauls-rollercoaster-ride-from-nastiest-family-feud-to-market-dominance/.
3. "How To Blow $9 Billion: The Fallen Stroh Family," *Forbes*, July 8, 2014, https://www.forbes.com/sites/kerryadolan/2014/07/08/how-the-stroh-family-lost-the-largest-private-beer-fortune-in-the-u-s/.

Chapter 8

1. Chris and Melissa Smith, interview with authors, February 3, 2026.

Chapter 9

1. Preston Troutt, interview with authors, January 15, 2026.
2. "Thomas Sowell: There Are No Solutions, Only Trade-offs," YouTube, accessed January 6, 2026, https://www.youtube.com/watch?v=3_EtIWmja-4.
3. Viktor E. Frankl, *Man's Search for Meaning* (Pocket Books, 1985), 68.

Chapter 10

1. [Name redacted], interview with authors, January 22, 2026.

Chapter 11

1. Melissa Osborn, interview with authors, January 20, 2026.
2. Walter Isaacson, *Steve Jobs* (Simon & Schuster, 2011), 430.

Chapter 12

1. "A Conversation: Yuval Noah Harari, Daniel Kahneman," Edge Foundation, March 4, 2015, https://www.edge.org/conversation/yuval_noah_harari-daniel_kahneman-death-is-optional.
2. "A Conversation," Edge Foundation.
3. Sir John Glubb, *The Fate of Empires and Search for Survival* (William Blackwood & Sons, 1976).
4. Samuel Arbesman, "The Life-Spans of Empires, Historical Methods," *A Journal of Quantitative and Interdisciplinary History* 44, no. 3 (2011): 127–129.

Index

A

B

C

D

E

F

G

H

I

J

K

L

M

R

S

T

U

V

W

Y

Z

About the Authors

Connor Boyack is a best-selling author of over fifty books and a trusted advisor to high-net-worth families on raising grounded, entrepreneurial creators. He is best known as the author of the acclaimed *Tuttle Twins* series, with more than seven million copies sold.

Connor is the founder and president of Libertas Network (see Libertas.org), a nonprofit that advances human flourishing through free-market education and real-world entrepreneurial experiences. With his team, he has changed more than one hundred laws, helped over one thousand young adults launch careers without a college degree, and helped over one hundred thousand children become entrepreneurs.

Learn more about him at ConnorBoyack.com.

Taylor Adams is an entrepreneur, investor, and coach who founded Belief Partners (see Belief.Partners) to help wealthy families navigate multigenerational wealth in a way that emphasizes purpose and meaning.

Based in Park City, Utah, he began his career in a Southern California family office as a fifth-generation family member, building expertise in alternative investments and later helping family offices design venture and venture-philanthropy platforms.